TRANSACTIONS
OF THE
ROYAL SOCIETY OF EDINBURGH.
VOL. XLIX.—PART II.—(No. 2).

THE ANTARCTIC FISHES OF THE SCOTTISH NATIONAL ANTARCTIC EXPEDITION.

BY

C. TATE REGAN, M.A.

[WITH ELEVEN PLATES AND SIX TEXT-FIGS.]

EDINBURGH:
PUBLISHED BY ROBERT GRANT & SON, 107 PRINCES STREET,
AND WILLIAMS & NORGATE, 14 HENRIETTA STREET, COVENT GARDEN, LONDON.

MDCCCCXIII.

Price Eight Shillings.

II.—**The Antarctic Fishes of the Scottish National Antarctic Expedition.** By C. Tate Regan, M.A., Assistant in the British Museum (Natural History). Communicated by Dr W. S. BRUCE. (With Eleven Plates and Six Text-figs.)

(MS. received June 18, 1912. Read December 16, 1912. Issued separately May 23, 1913.)

Our knowledge of the Antarctic fish-fauna has greatly increased during the last ten years. The Belgian expedition to Graham Land (1897–1899) was followed by that of the *Southern Cross* to Victoria Land (1898–1900), fitted out by Sir GEORGE NEWNES. Next were the British expedition of the *Discovery* to Victoria Land and Edward Land (1901–1904), the German voyage of the *Gauss* to Kerguelen and Wilhelm Land (1901–1903), and NORDENSKJOLD'S Swedish expedition to South Georgia, the South Shetlands, and Graham Land. Then came the voyage of the *Scotia* to the South Orkneys and Coats Land (1902–1904), and CHARCOT'S expeditions to the Palmer Archipelago and Graham Land in the *Français* (1904–1905) and the *Pourquoi Pas?* (1908–1910), and finally SHACKLETON'S expedition (1908–1909).

The fishes collected during these expeditions have been described in a series of reports, which may be enumerated in chronological order:—

> 1903 BOULENGER, *Pisces* in "*Southern Cross*" *Collections*, pp. 174–189, pls. xi–xviii.
> 1904 DOLLO *R.s. Voy "Belgica"* Poissons, 240 pp., 12 pls.
> 1905 LÖNNBERG, "The Fishes of the Swedish South Polar Expedition," *Wissensch. Ergebn. Schwedisch. Sudpolar-Exped.*, v. 6, 69 pp., 5 pls.
> 1906 VAILLANT, *Exped. Antarct. Française* Poissons, 51 pp.
> 1907 BOULENGER *National Antarctic Expedition*, *Nat. Hist.* II, Fishes, 5 pp., 2 pls.
> 1911 WAITE "Antarctic Fishes" in *British Antarctic Expedition*, 1907–9 *Biology*, pp. 11–16, pl. ii.
> 1912 PAPPENHEIM, 'Die Fische der Antarktis und Subantarktis," in *Deutsche Sudpolar-Exped.*, 1901–1903 XIII, *Zool.* v. pp. 163–182, pls. ix–x.

Dr DOLLO presented several preliminary notes in the *Proceedings of the Royal Society of Edinburgh*[*] on the fishes of the Scottish National Antarctic Expedition.

The fishes of the second Charcot expedition have been worked out by Professor ROULE, who has published two preliminary notes (*C.R. Acad. Sci. Paris*, clii., 1911, pp. 80–81, and *Bull. Mus. Paris*, 1911, pp. 276–281), but the final report has not yet appeared.

The important collection of fishes here reported on was made at the Falkland Islands, the South Orkneys, Coats Land, and Gough Island, and in the Weddell Sea and South Atlantic Ocean between these localities. As will be seen from the systematic list that follows, it includes examples of forty-eight species, ten of which are now described as new to science, whilst three others, known before but wrongly identified, are diagnosed and given new specific names. In addition, four species have already been described by

---

[*] *Proc. Roy. Soc. Edin.*, xxvi, 1906, p. 172; xxviii, 1908, p. 58; xxix, 1909, p. 316.

Di Dollo, in whose hands the greater part of the collection has been from 1905 until March 1912.

The identification of the Notothenioids and Zoarcids has proved a difficult matter in the present state of our knowledge of these groups, and I have supplemented my report by a monograph of the former and a revision of the southern genera of the latter; further, I have added some notes on the Galaxiidæ and Haplochitonidæ, as their distribution has given rise to some discussion.

My work on the Notothenioids and Zoarcids is mainly based on the specimens in the British Museum, including the *Erebus* and *Terror*, *Challenger*, *Southern Cross* and *Discovery* collections, but I have been greatly helped by the loan of specimens from the Museums at Paris, Berlin and Stockholm. Thus I have been able to examine all the species of *Notothenia* recorded by VAILLANT from Graham Land, two of the three species of Zoarcids recently described by PAPPENHEIM from Wilhelm Land, and co-types of some of the Notothenioids described by LÖNNBERG. For their kindness in sending me these fishes, and in giving me information about others that could not be sent, I heartily thank Dr PELLEGRIN, Dr PAPPENHEIM, and Dr LÖNNBERG.

It need hardly be said that the fishes lend no support to the theory of bipolarity. Most of the littoral fishes belong to the Notothenidæ and related families, which are characteristic of and peculiar to the Antarctic seas and the region immediately to the north of them; there are also several species of Zoarcidæ, generically distinct from the northern members of the family. Some of the pelagic and abyssal fishes are Notothenioids peculiar to the Antarctic region; others also such as *Notolepis*, *Cynomacrurus*, and *Eugnathosaurus*, may not be found elsewhere; but the rest belong to widely distributed genera (*Synaphobranchus*, *Bathylagus*, *Myctophum*, etc.) or even species (e.g. *Cyclothone microdon*).

In the whole paper the following seven new genera and twenty-one new species are described:—

NEW GENERA

Eugnathosaurus, p. 234
Ophthalmolycus, p. 243
Austrolycichthys, p. 244
Austrolycus, p. 245

Crossolycus, p. 247
Pogetopsis, p. 286
Chænocephalus, p. 287

NEW SPECIES

Bathylagus glacialis, p. 231
Eugnathosaurus vorax, p. 234
Synaphobranchus australis, p. 235
Chalinura ferrieri, p. 236
„ whitsoni, p. 236
Cæsioperca coatsi, p. 237
Neophynchthys marmoratus, p. 241
Lycenchelys antarcticus, p. 242
Austrolycus depressiceps, p. 245
Crossolycus chilensis, p. 247
Cottoperca macrophthalma, p. 253

Bovichthys angustifrons, p. 255
„ chilensis, p. 256
„ decipiens, p. 257
Trematomus loennbergi, p. 263
Notothenia trigramma, p. 266
„ ramsayi, p. 267
„ williami, p. 268
„ vaillanti, p. 272
Chænichthys rugosus, p. 287
Cygodraco pappenheimi, p. 289

1. ANTARCTIC AND SUBANTARCTIC FISHES COLLECTED BY THE "SCOTIA"*

SELACHII

RAIDÆ

1. *Raia magellanica*, Steind. (Pl. I.)

   Zool. Jahrb. Suppl., vi., 1905, p. 212.

One specimen from Station 346, Burdwood Bank, depth 56 fathoms, taken on 1st December 1905. Lat. 54° 25' S., long. 57° 32' W., temperature 41.8° F.

This is a female of exactly the same size as STEINDACHNER'S type, and apparently in every way similar, except that there is only a single scapulary spine, instead of a series of three on each side.

This species is related to *R. murrayi*, Gunth., from Kerguelen, but has a blunter snout, a shorter tail and somewhat different spination.

ISOSPONDYLI

CLUPEIDÆ

2. *Clupea fuegensis*, Jenyns.

   Zool. "Beagle," Fish., p. 133 (1842); Smitt, *Bihang Svensk. Vet. Akad.*, xxiv., 1898, iv., No 5 p. 59, pl. v. fig. 41.

Depth of body 4 to 5 in the length. Lower jaw very prominent; minute teeth in a single series on the palatines and in an elongate patch on the tongue. Dorsal 17-18, origin equidistant from anterior edge of eye and base of caudal fin. Anal 17-20. Origin of pelvics vertically below that of dorsal. About 50 scales in a longitudinal series; ventral scutes not prominent.

Several specimens, up to 170 mm. in total length, taken at Station 118, Port Stanley, Falkland Islands, in February 1904, when extraordinary shoals of this herring visited Port Stanley Harbour.

ARGENTINIDÆ

3. *Bathylagus glacialis*, sp. n. (Pl. IX. fig. 2.)

Depth of body 6 to 6½ in the length; length of head 4⅛ to 4½. Diameter of eye 2⅕ to 2⅓ in the length of head; interocular width 3, interorbital width 6. Dorsal 10, origin nearer to end of snout than to base of caudal. Anal 18. Pelvics 8-rayed, inserted below middle of dorsal. About 35 scales in a longitudinal series.

---

* A series of nine water-colour drawings made by Mr CUTHBERTSON for the most part represent fishes from Scotia Bay, South Orkneys, viz. *Notolepis coatsi*, *Harpagifer bispinis*, *Trematomus newnesi*, *Notothenia coriiceps*, *N. nudifrons*, and *N. gibberifrons*; there is also a sketch of *Lycenchelys antarcticus*. In one or two cases I have referred to these in the text.

There are five examples of this new species, 70 to 100 mm. in total length:—

1. Station 398, 68° 25′ S., 27° 10′ W., 1 to 1000 fathoms, surface temperature 30° F., vertical net, 29th February 1904.
2. Station 422, 68° 32′ S., 12° 49′ W., 0 to 800 fathoms, surface temperature 31·1° F., temperature at 800 fathoms 32·4° F., vertical net, 23rd March 1904.
3. Station 414, 71° 50′ S., 23° 30′ W., 0 to 1000 fathoms, surface temperature 29·1° F., vertical net, 15th March 1904.
4. Station 417, 71° 22′ S., 16° 34′ W., 1410 fathoms, temperature at 1410 fathoms 31·9° F., trawl, 18th March 1904.
5. Station 418, 71° 32′ S., 17° 15′ W., 1221 fathoms, temperature at 1221 fathoms 31·9° F., trawl, 19th March 1904.

Bathylagus antarcticus Gunth., is distinguished by the less graceful form (depth 5 in the length) and the longer anal fin with 22 rays. *Bathylagus gracilis*, another Antarctic species recently described by LÖNNBERG, has the interorbital space very narrow and deeply concave and about 41 scales in a longitudinal series.

Other species of *Bathylagus* have been described from the South Atlantic (GUNTHER, LÖNNBERG), the North Atlantic (GOODE and BEAN), and the North Pacific (GILBERT).

GALAXIIDÆ

4. *Galaxias attenuatus* Jenyns

Two examples from Port Stanley and Port Harriet, Falkland Islands, Station 118.

5. *Galaxias maculatus*, Jenyns

Several from Port Harriet, Station 118.

HAPLOCHITONIDÆ

6. *Haplochiton zebra*, Jenyns

One specimen from Port Stanley, Falkland Islands, in fresh water, Station 118.

STOMIATIDÆ

7. *Stomias boa*, Risso

One from Station 451, 48° 06′ S., 10° 5′ W., 1742 fathoms, trawl, 13th April 1904.

8. *Cyclothone microdon*, Gunth.

Small examples of this widely distributed species were taken at three stations, viz.:—

- Six at Station 450, 48° 00′ S., 9° 50′ W., 1332 fathoms, surface temperature 40·0° F., trawl, 13th April 1904.
- One at Station 422, 68° 32′ S., 12° 49′ W., 0–800 fathoms, temperature at 800 fathoms 32·4° F., vertical net, 23rd March 1904.
- Four at Station 414, 71° 50′ S., 23° 30′ W., 0–1000 fathoms, surface temperature 29·1° F., vertical net, 15th March 1904.

INIOMI
SUDIDÆ
9. *Notolepis coatsii*, Dollo

Proc. Roy. Soc. Edin., xxviii., 1908, p. 58
Prymnothonus (part.), Günth., '*Challenger*' *Pelagic Fish*, p. 39, pl. v. fig. D (1889)
  „   *Hookeri* (non Richards.), Dollo, *Proc. Roy. Soc. Edin.*, xxvii., 1907, p. 35

Depth of body $6\frac{1}{2}$ in the length; length of head 5.; snout half the length of head; diameter of eye $6\frac{1}{2}$ in the length of head. Teeth rather small, pointed, uniserial, in jaws and on palatines. Dorsal 8., origin nearly equidistant from head and base of caudal; adipose fin rather long and low. Anal 28. Caudal with numerous procurrent rays. Pectorals narrow, about $\frac{1}{4}$ length of head. Vent below anterior part of dorsal. Scales deciduous. Myotomes 82, 34 in advance of dorsal fin. Silvery white, back bluish.

It is with some difficulty that I have put together the above description of the type of the species, 105 mm. in total length, taken at the surface in Scotia Bay, South Orkneys. The specimen is in very bad condition,* and everything that one touches falls off, hence it is not surprising that I cannot see the small pelvic fins described by Dollo.

In a paper on the classification of the Iniomi (*Ann. Mag. Nat. Hist.* (8), vii., 1911, pp. 120-133) I have already called attention to the fact that Dollo's family *Paralepidæ* is not a natural group, and that *Notolepis* differs from *Paralepis* apparently only in the greater length of the adipose fin; a character of very slight importance to anyone familiar with the species of Siluroids.

Larval and post-larval examples of this species that I have examined are:—

1.—44 mm., 62° 26' S., 95° 44' E. *Challenger* collection.
2.—50 mm., at Station 422, 68° 32' S., 12° 49' W., 10-800 fathoms, temperature at 800 fathoms 32.4° F., 23rd March 1904. *Scotia* collection.
3-5.—38 to 56 mm., at Station 414, 71° 50' S., 33° 30' W., 0-1000 fathoms, surface temperature 29.1° F., 15th March 1904. *Scotia* collection.

Except that the teeth are relatively stronger and the eye larger, specimens 1 and 2 are extremely similar to the type, and agree with it in the number of fin-rays and of myotomes; I cannot find any pelvic fins, nor ascertain the position of the vent, but the eight-rayed dorsal fin is distinct in both.

Specimens 3 to 5 are the ones described by Dollo as *Prymnothonus hookeri*; these evidently belong to the same species as the other examples, with which the larger one agrees in the head, dentition, and approximate number of myotomes. In the smaller ones the head is relatively smaller and the snout shorter. I am unable to make out the fins, or position of vent, and I am very doubtful as to whether the so-called embryonic anal fringe is an actual structure present in the living fish.

Dr Dollo named this species in honour of the late Mr James Coats, junr., of Paisley, whose generosity was the chief means of assuring the dispatch of the Scottish National Antarctic Expedition.

* This is regrettable, as this specimen was originally so perfectly preserved and was brought home in perfect condition, and was acknowledged to have been received by Dr Dollo "*en bon etat*."—W. S. B., Editor.

MYCTOPHIDÆ

10. *Myctophum antarcticum*, Günth.

Specimens were taken at

Station 309. 63° 51′ S., 41° 50′ W., 2300 fathoms, temperature 31·05° F. trawl, 16th March 1903.

Station 414. 71° 50′ S., 23° 30′ W., 0–1000 fathoms, surface temperature 29·1° F. vertical net, 15th March 1904.

Station 422. 68° 32′ S., 12° 49′ W., 0–800 fathoms, surface temperature 32·7° F., temperature at 800 fathoms 32·4°, vertical net, 23rd March 1904.

11. *Lampanyctus braueri*, Lönnberg.

One specimen was taken at Station 420, lat. 69° 33′ S., 15° 19′ W., 2620 fathoms, by the trawl, on 21st March 1904, temperature 31·5° F. The species was previously known only from the type.

ALEPIDOSAURIDÆ

Eugnathosaurus gen. nov.

Skull very elongate and strongly compressed, with the upper surface somewhat convex, bearing a fairly prominent median ridge. Snout and lower jaw much produced, each ending in a fleshy appendage; lower jaw projecting beyond upper suspensorium directed obliquely forward. Teeth pointed, uniserial, premaxillary teeth minute, mandibulary teeth sub-conical erect or somewhat retrorse, strongest in the middle of the length of the jaw, more spaced posteriorly; palatine teeth strong, compressed, curved somewhat forward.

12. *Eugnathosaurus vorax*, sp. n.

The type of this remarkable new genus and species is a head measuring 150 mm. in length from tip of snout to end of operculum taken in the trawl on 18th March 1904,

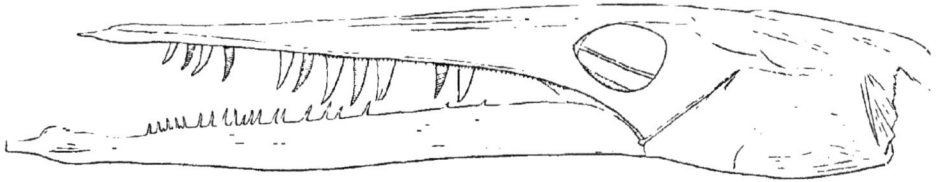

FIG. 1.—*Eugnathosaurus vorax*.

at Station 417, in lat. 71° 22′ S., long. 16° 34′ W., off Coats Land at a depth of 1410 fathoms, by the trawl, temp. 31·9° F. That it is related to *Alepidosaurus* is evident, but the form of the skull, the produced jaws and the different mandibulary and palatine dentition distinguish it from that genus, the antrorse palatine teeth are especially peculiar

The dentaries of a second specimen were taken at the same locality

APODES

SYNAPHOBRANCHIDÆ

13 *Synaphobranchus australis*, sp n   (Pl VIII fig 5)

Synaphobranchus bathybius (part), Gunth, ' *Challenger* " *Deep Sea Fish*, p 254 (1887)

The *Challenger* specimen, 350 mm in total length, was taken midway between the Cape of Good Hope and Kerguelen at a depth of 1375 fathoms. The *Scotia* example was obtained on 13th April 1904, at Station 451, in 48° 06' S, 10° 5' W, at a depth of 1742 fathoms, and measures a total length of 470 mm. The species belongs to the sub-genus *Histiobranchus*, Gill, which includes also *S bathybius*, Gunth and *S infernalis*, Gill. All three are closely related, differing as follows —

Eye nearer to end of snout than to angle of mouth, origin of dorsal above base of pectoral its distance from end of snout rather less than $\frac{1}{2}$ that from end of snout to vent   *bathybius*

Eye about equidistant from snout and angle of mouth, origin of dorsal above posterior part of pectoral, its distance from end of snout somewhat more than $\frac{1}{2}$ that from end of snout to vent   *infernalis*

Eye about equidistant from snout and angle of mouth, origin of dorsal a little behind end of pectoral its distance from end of snout about $2\frac{1}{4}$ in that from end of snout to vent   *australis*

ANACANTHINI

MACRURIDÆ

Four species of this family were obtained by the *Scotia* in Antarctic seas, all belonging to the sub-family *Macrurinæ* (cf *Ann Mag Nat Hist* (7), xi, 1903, pp 459–466), and to genera with the teeth in the lower jaw uniserial

14 *Nematonurus lecointei*, Dollo

Rés Voy "Belgica" Poiss, p 44 pl vii (1904), *Proc Roy Soc Edin*, xxv 1909, p 488

The type was taken in 70° 40' S, 102° 15' W, depth 1526 fathoms. The *Scotia* examples are from (1) Station 313, 62° 10' S, 41° 20' W 1775 fathoms temperature 31 0° F, trawl, 18th March 1903   (2) Station 451, 48° 06' S, 10° 05' W, 1742 fathoms, 13th April 1904

The præmaxillary teeth are biserial except posteriorly, where the inner series is replaced by three, forming a narrow band

15. *Chalinura ferrieri*, sp. n. (Pl. II. fig. 1.)

Snout rather strongly produced (for a *Chalinura*), mouth wide, the maxillary nearly reaching the vertical from posterior edge of eye, infraorbital ridge fairly prominent. Diameter of eye less than length of snout, $4\frac{2}{3}$ in length of head; interorbital width 4. Dorsal II 9, distance from second dorsal a little more than $\frac{2}{3}$ the length of head. Origin of anal at distance from head equal to length of head without snout. Pectoral 18 or 19-rayed, $\frac{3}{4}$ the length of head, extending to above origin of anal. Pelvics 11-rayed, the outermost ray filamentous, reaching anal. Scales mostly with 3 parallel series of spinules, but the lateral series sometimes reduced to a single spine, or absent. 8 scales between dorsal fin and lateral line.

A single specimen, 230 mm. in total length, from Station 417, 71° 22′ S., 16° 34′ W., 1410 fathoms, off Coats Land, temperature at 1400 fathoms 31.9° F., trawl, 18th March 1904.

This species is named after JAMES G. FERRIER, Esq., F.R.S.G.S., Hon. Secretary of the *Scotia* Committee.

16. *Chalinura whitsoni*, sp. n. (Pl. II. fig. 2.)

Snout rather produced (for a *Chalinura*), maxillary extending to below posterior margin of pupil; infraorbital ridge prominent. Diameter of eye more than length of snout, $2\frac{3}{4}$ to $3\frac{1}{4}$ in length of head; interorbital width 4 to $4\frac{1}{2}$. Dorsal II 9–10, distance from second dorsal $\frac{1}{4}$ the length of head. Origin of anal at distance from head equal to length of head without snout. Pectoral 18–19-rayed. Pelvic 9-rayed, the outermost ray filamentous, not reaching anal. Scales with 1 series of spinules, but some on sides of head with 3 series converging anteriorly; 7 scales between dorsal fin and lateral line.

Two specimens:—

1. 420 mm., Station 451, 48° 6′ S., 10° 5′ W., 1742 fathoms, trawl, 13th April 1904.
2. 270 mm., Station 417, 71° 22′ S., 16° 34′ W., 1410 fathoms, off Coats Land, temperature at 1400 fathoms 31.9° F., trawl, 18th March 1904.

This species is named after T. B. WHITSON, Esq., C.A., Hon. Accountant of the *Scotia* Committee.

17. *Cynomacrurus piriei*, Dollo. (Pl. III. fig. 1.)

Proc. Roy. Soc. Edin., xxix., 1909, p. 316.

The type of the genus and species, a specimen of 300 mm., was obtained by the *Scotia* at Station 414, 71° 50′ S., 23° 30′ W., in a depth 0–1000 fathoms, surface temperature 31.5° F., vertical net, on 15th February 1904. The dentition is very characteristic; in the præmaxillaries a narrow band of unequal teeth separated by an interspace from a marginal series of small teeth with a strong pair of antero-lateral canines, in the lower jaw teeth strong, spaced, unequal uniserial

Other important characters are the large terminal mouth with lateral cleft, the absence of a barbel, the small eye, and the slender, smooth dorsal spine. The pelvic fins are 7-rayed, and in counting 12 Dr Dollo must have reckoned divided rays as two.

This species was named by Dr Dollo after Dr J. H. Harvey Pirie, bacteriologist, geologist, and surgeon of the *Scotia*.

PERCOMORPHI

SERRANIDÆ

18. *Cænoperca coatsii*, sp. n. (Pl VI fig 1)

Depth of body $2\frac{2}{3}$ to $3\frac{1}{4}$ in the length, length of head $2\frac{3}{4}$ to 3. Diameter of eye $2\frac{1}{3}$ to $2\frac{2}{3}$ in length of head, interorbital width $4\frac{1}{3}$ to 5. Interorbital region flat, maxillary extending to below middle of eye, 21 to 24 gill-rakers on lower part of anterior arch. Dorsal X, 15–18, third or fourth spine longest, nearly twice as long as last, $\frac{2}{3}$ to $\frac{1}{2}$ length of head. Anal III 8, second spine longest, as long as or longer than longest dorsal spine. Pectoral shorter than head, asymmetrical, the rays increasing to the tenth counting from above, or seventh, from below. Caudal truncate. About 40 scales in a lateral longitudinal series and 45 in the lateral line which forms an angle on the caudal peduncle. Pale reddish brown, with traces of alternating darker and paler longitudinal bands; upper half of spinous dorsal blackish, or with a series of blackish spots.

Gough Island. Several specimens, up to 135 mm in total length, taken at Station 461, 40° 20′ S, 9° 56′ W, off Gough Island, at a depth of 100 fathoms, surface temperature 54.5° F, trawl, 23rd April 1904.

This species is of considerable interest as its three congeners are found on the coasts of South Australia, Tasmania, and New Zealand. These are distinguished by their longer pectoral and emarginate caudal fins, and by the convex interorbital region; but I am unable to find any characters which would justify the establishment of a new genus for the new species. The pectoral fin of *C. rasor* is almost as asymmetrical, and I find that the flatness of the interorbital region of *C. coatsii* is not associated with any difference in the essential structure of the frontal bones, which are, as in *C. lepidoptera*, smooth and convex posteriorly, and anteriorly consist of a pair of supraorbital flanges and of a median depression bordered by muciferous canals.

I have pleasure in naming this species after Major Andrew Coats, D.S.O., a member of the *Scotia* Committee, a most generous donor to the funds of the Scottish National Antarctic Expedition, and himself a polar explorer.

ATHERINIDÆ

19. *Basilichthys laticlavia*, Cuv. and Val.

Several small specimens from Station 118, Port Stanley Harbour, Falkland Islands, 51° 41′ S, 57° 51′ W, shore.

ZOARCIDÆ

20. *Ilucates fimbriatus*, Jenyns

Station 118, Port Stanley, Falkland Islands, 51° 41′ S., 57° 51′ W., shore.

21. *Austrolycus depressiceps*, Regan

Several small specimens from Station 118, Port Stanley, Falkland Islands, 51° 41′ S., 57° 51′ W., shore. This species is described on p. 245.

22. *Phucocates latitans*, Jenyns

Four small specimens from Station 118, Port Stanley, Falkland Islands, 51° 41′ S., 57° 51′ W., shore.

23. *Lycenchelys antarcticus*, Regan

This new species is described on p. 242 from a single specimen from Station 313, 62° 10′ S., 41° 20′ W., depth 1775 fathoms, temperature 31.0° F., trawl, 18th March 1903.

BROTULIDÆ

24. *Neobythites brucei*, Dollo. (Pl. III. fig. 2.)

Proc. Roy. Soc. Edin., xxvi, 1906, p. 172.

Depth of body 6½ in the length, length of head 5, or 1⅔ in its distance from origin of anal. Diameter of eye 1.3 in length of head, equal to width of posterior nostril; maxillary extending well behind eye; palatine bands of teeth broad; no præopercular spines; gill-membranes united for a short distance to each other and to isthmus; 15 gill-rakers on lower part of anterior arch. About 125 scales in a longitudinal series. Dorsal 108, origin behind base of pectoral. Anal 86. Pectoral nearly as long as head; pelvics ⅔ the length of head, 2-rayed, each ray simple, expanded distally into an ovate blade.

The type, 350 mm. in total length, was taken at Station 291, 67° 33′ S., 36° 35′ W., depth 2500 fathoms; trawl, 7th March 1903.

From most species of *Neobythites* this species differs in the gill-membranes attached to the isthmus and the oar-shaped pelvic rays, and I should be inclined to recognise GARMAN's genus *Holcomycteronus* for this species and *N. digittatus*, had not GARMAN stated that the form of the pelvic rays is variable in the latter.

This species was named by Dr. DOLLO after Dr. W. S. BRUCE, leader of the Scottish National Antarctic Expedition.

BOVICHTHYIDÆ

25. *Cottoperca gobio*, Gunth.

Station 349, 51° 41′ S., 57° 51′ W., Port William, Falkland Islands, shore.

26 *Cottoperca macrophthalma*, Regan

At Station 346 54° 25′ S, 57° 32′ W Burdwood Bank, 56 fathoms, surface temperature 41 8° F, otter trawl, 1st December 1903 This new species is described on p 253

27 *Bovichthys diacanthus*, Carmich

A specimen of 120 mm from Gough Island On comparison with Chilian examples of the species usually known as *B diacanthus* I find that they are distinct (cf p 256)

NOTOTHENIIDÆ

28 *Harpagifer bispinis*, Forst

Several examples from Station 118, Port Stanley, Falkland Islands, and Station 325, Scotia Bay, South Orkneys—the latter a new record of locality for this species

29 *Trematomus newnesii*, Bouleng

Station 325, Scotia Bay, South Orkneys

30 *Trematomus borchgrevinki*, Bouleng

Station 325, Scotia Bay, South Orkneys

31 *Trematomus bernacchii*, Bouleng

Station 325, South Orkneys

32 *Trematomus hansoni*, Bouleng

Station 411, Coats Land, 161 fathoms

33 *Notothenia trigramma*, Regan

This new species, from Station 118, at the Falkland Islands, is described on p 266

34 *Notothenia ramsayi*, Regan

This new species, from Station 346, the Burdwood Bank is described on p 267

35 *Notothenia tesselata*, Richards

Station 118, Port Stanley, Falkland Islands

36 *Notothenia wiltoni* Regan

Examples of this new species, described on p 268, were taken by the *Scotia* at Station 118, Port Stanley, Falklands, and at Station 346, the Burdwood Bank

37 *Notothenia brevicauda*, Lonnb

Station 118, Port Stanley, Falkland Islands

38. *Notothenia sima*, Richards.

Station 118, Port Stanley, Falkland Islands.

39. *Notothenia gibberifrons*, Lönnb.

Station 325, Scotia Bay, South Orkneys.

40. *Notothenia nudifrons*, Lönnb.

Station 325, Scotia Bay, South Orkneys.

41. *Notothenia coriiceps*, Richards.

South Orkneys, common at Station 325, Scotia Bay.

42. *Notothenia cornucola*, Richards.

Station 118, Port Stanley, Falkland Islands.

43. *Notothenia rossii*, Richards.

Station 325, Scotia Bay, South Orkneys.

44. *Eleginops maclovinus*, Cuv. and Val.

Station 118, Port Stanley, Falkland Islands.

BATHYDRACONIDÆ

45. *Bathydraco scotiæ*, Dollo.

Station 417, 71° 22′ S., 16° 34′ W., off Coats Land, at a depth of 1410 fathoms. This species is described on p. 282.

SCLEROPAREI

SCORPÆNIDÆ

46. *Sebastes maculatus*, Cuv. and Val.

Specimens from Station 461, Gough Island at 25 fathoms and 100 fathoms, the latter with *Caesioperca coatsi*.

47. *Sebastes capensis*, Gmel.

A small specimen taken at Station 461, Gough Island with the preceding; both these species are found at the Cape of Good Hope.

PSYCHROLUTIDÆ

48 Neophrynichthys marmoratus, sp. n.

Neophrynichthys latus (non Hutton), Günth., Proc. Zool. Soc., 1881, p. 20, pl. i.

In this species the dermal appendages on the head and anterior part of the body are much larger and set further apart than in *N. latus*. Another striking difference is the narrower interorbital region, its width measuring only ¼ of the length of the head in *N. marmoratus*, but ⅔ in its congener from New Zealand. The dorsal rays number IX–X, 15–16, the anal 11 or 12, the caudal is more rounded than in *N. latus*.

The irregular marbling gives this fish a very different appearance from the New Zealand form, with its definite pale spots separated by a brown network.

Three specimens, two in the British Museum collection, from the Straits of Magellan, 320 and 390 mm. in total length, and one of 160 mm. obtained by the *Scotia* at Station 346, 54° 25′ S., 57° 32′ W., Burdwood Bank, 56 fathoms, surface temperature 41.8° F., otter trawl, 1st December 1903.

II. A REVISION OF THE ZOARCIDÆ OF SOUTHERN AMERICA AND THE ANTARCTIC

The Zoarcidæ are principally a northern family and so far as I am aware none is known from South Africa, Australia or New Zealand. Two northern deep-water genera, *Lycenchelys* and *Melanostigma*, are represented in the Antarctic Regions, but the littoral species, with those of South America and the adjacent islands, all belong to genera distinct from the northern ones.* There has hitherto been much confusion as to the characters of these genera and species, which it is the object of this revision to clear up.

Synopsis of the Genera

I. Pelvic fins present, mouth subterminal
   A. Snout and lower jaw without fringes
      1. Origin of dorsal fin well behind base of pectoral, gill-opening cleft downward nearly or quite to lower end of base of pectoral.
         Teeth uniserial or biserial in jaws, uniserial on palatines, tail long and slender . . . . 1. *Lycenchelys*
         Teeth in jaws triserial, two teeth near anterior end of each palatine, tail moderately elongate . . . . 2. *Ophthalmolycus*
      2. Origin of dorsal fin above base or anterior part of pectoral, gill-opening cleft downward at least to middle of base of pectoral.
         a. Mouth large with wide lateral cleft, gill opening cleft downwards almost or quite to lower end of base of pectoral, teeth in jaws uniserial, with anterior canines in the upper and lateral canines in the lower.

---
* The habitat of *Gymnelis pictus*, Günth., is unknown, and there is no justification whatever for the statement that it comes from Magellan Straits.

Teeth on vomer and palatines .... 3 *Iluocœtes*
Palate toothless .... 4 *Lycodichthys*
  b Mouth moderate, with short lateral cleft, teeth in jaws
    uniserial laterally, usually bi- or tri-serial anteriorly, no
    well marked canines, teeth on palate
    Head not depressed, gill-opening cleft downward nearly to lower end of
      base of pectoral .... 5 *Austrolycichthys*
    Head depressed, gill-opening cleft downward only to middle of base of
      pectoral .... 6 *Austrolycus*
  3 Origin of dorsal fin above base of pectoral, gill opening small,
    above the pectoral, teeth in upper jaw uniserial, in lower bi-
    or tri-serial, teeth on palate .... 7 *Phucocœtes*
B Snout and lower jaw with dermal fringes, palate toothless
  Teeth conical, bi- or tri-serial, gill-opening almost entirely above the
    pectoral .... 8 *Crossolycus*
  Teeth incisor-like, uniserial, gill-opening cleft downward to middle of
    base of pectoral .... 9 *Platea*
II No pelvic fins, mouth terminal, origin of dorsal just behind head, teeth
  uniserial, in jaws and on vomer and palatines
  Gill-opening cleft downward to middle of base of pectoral .... 10 *Maynea*
  Gill opening above base of pectoral .... 11 *Melanostigma*

1 *Lycenchelys*, Gill, 1884

Proc. Acad Philad, p 110

Form elongate, with the tail long and slender, mouth subterminal, teeth in jaws slender, uni- or bi-serial, teeth on vomer, palatine teeth uniserial. Gill opening rather wide, cleft downwards to lower end of base of pectoral. Dorsal origin well behind head, pelvic fins present

Lycenchelys antarcticus, sp n (Pl IX fig 3)

Depth of body 16 in the length, length of head 6 and equal to its distance from origin of anal fin. Head as broad as deep, its breadth a little more than ½ its length. Snout twice as long as diameter of eye, which is 6 in length of head. interorbital width about 10. Muciferous channels of sides of head and lower jaw with large pores. Lower jaw included, teeth in jaws rather slender and obtuse, uniserial, biserial near symphysis of lower jaw, teeth on palate acute, wide-set. About 110 rays in dorsal fin, 9 in caudal, 103 in anal, origin of anal ⅓ as distant from vertical through origin of dorsal as from that through base of pectoral, which fin is a little more than ½ as long as head. Bluish grey, head darker, fins brownish grey

A single specimen, 128 mm in total length, from near the South Orkneys, Station

313, 62° 10′ S., 41° 20′ W., depth 1775 fathoms, bottom temperature 31 0° F., trawl 18th March 1903

The few species of this genus hitherto described are from deep water north of the Equator

2 *Ophthalmolycus*, gen nov

Form elongate, compressed Mouth subterminal, teeth rather slender and acute, in about 3 series in both jaws, no canines, 3 teeth on vomer and 2 near anterior end of each palatine Gill-opening rather wide, cleft downwards nearly to lower end of base of pectoral Dorsal origin well behind head, pelvic fins present

Ophthalmolycus macrops

Lycodes macrops, Günth, '*Challenger*" *Shore Fish*, p 21, pl xi fig B (1880)

Depth of body $11\frac{1}{2}$ in the length, length of head $5\frac{1}{4}$. Diameter of eye $3\frac{1}{3}$ in length of head and 7 times interorbital width Maxillary nearly reaching vertical from posterior margin of eye About 90 rays in the dorsal fin, 80 in the anal, and 10 in the caudal Origin of dorsal above posterior $\frac{1}{4}$ of pectoral origin of anal a head-length behind the head Pectoral less than $\frac{1}{2}$ the length of head Yellowish, 9 broad dark-brown cross-bars on back, extending on to dorsal fin, a series of brown spots on the side, alternating with the bars, a brown band from eye to operculum

Straits of Magellan, 40 to 140 fathoms

Here described from the type, 135 mm in total length

Lycodes concolor, Roule (*Bull Mus Paris*, 1911, p 280) may belong to this genus D 73, A 68 Coloration uniform

3 *Iluocœtes* Jenyns, 1842

Zool "Beagle," Fish, p 165

Head about as broad as deep, body compressed, mouth subterminal, with wide lateral cleft, teeth conical, uniserial in jaws in a patch on the vomer and a single series on the palatines, 1 or 2 pairs of canines at the symphysis of the upper jaw, 1 or 2 teeth on each side of lower jaw enlarged, canine-like Gill-opening cleft downward to lower end of base of pectoral Dorsal origin just behind head, pelvic fins present

Iluocœtes fimbriatus

Jenyns, *t c*, p 166, pl xxix fig 2
Lycodes variegatus, Günth, *Cat Fish*, iv p 322 (1868)
Phucocœtes variegatus effusus, Smitt, *Bihang Svensk Vet -Akad*, xxiv 1898, iv, No 5, p 43, pl v fig 32
Phucocœtes variegatus micropus, Smitt, *l c*, pl v fig 33

Depth of body 8 to $11\frac{1}{4}$ in the length, length of head $4\frac{1}{2}$ to $5\frac{1}{4}$. Diameter of eye 4 to $5\frac{1}{2}$ in length of head, 3 or 4 times the interorbital width Maxillary extending to below posterior margin of eye Dorsal with 80 to 85 rays, anal with 65 to 70 caudal with about 10. Origin of dorsal above base of pectoral, of anal about a head-length behind head. Pectoral ⅔ to ⅔ the length of head. Head, body, and fins spotted and marbled, sometimes cross-bars on the body; a more or less distinct band from snout to eye and eye to operculum; a series of blackish spots at margin of dorsal and anal.

Falkland Islands, Magellan Straits, Chile.

Here described from specimens from the Falkland Islands 80 to 130 mm. in total length, including the types of *Lycodes variegatus* and two obtained by the *Scotia* at Station 118, Port Stanley.

I am indebted to Mr. L. Doncaster for the loan of Jenyns's type; the appearance of some of the mucous canals as free fringing tubes is due to the bad state of preservation of the specimen.

Smitt's *Phucocœtes variegatus elongatus* (*t.c.*, p. 44, pl. v. fig. 34) seems to be a distinct species, with the head ⅓ of the distance from operculum to origin of anal.

4. *Lycodichthys*, Pappenheim, 1911.

Sitzungsb. Gesellsch. Naturf. Freunde, 1911, p. 382.

Closely related to *Iluocœtes*, differing especially in the toothless palate, teeth uniserial, anterior pair in upper jaw enlarged, lateral teeth of lower jaw spaced, canine-like.

Lycodichthys antarcticus.

Pappenheim, *t.c.*, p. 383, and *Deutsche Südpolar-Exped.*, xiii., *Zool.*, v. p. 180, pls. ix. fig. 6 and x. fig. 4.

Depth of body 8 or 9 in the length; length of head 5 to 5½. Diameter of eye 5 to 6 in length of head. Maxillary extending to below posterior margin of eye or a little beyond. Dorsal with 85 to 90 rays, anal with about 65, caudal with about 10. Origin of dorsal a little behind base of pectoral, of anal 1 to 1¼ head-lengths behind head. Pectoral ½ the length of head. Head, body, and fins spotted or marbled.

Wilhelm Land.

Here described from two co-types, 160 and 200 mm. in total length.

5. *Austrolycichthys*, gen. nov.

Closely related to *Austrolycus*, differing in the more compressed form, the head being at least as deep as broad, and in the more inferiorly placed and somewhat larger gill-openings, cleft downward nearly to the lower ends of the bases of the pectorals.

(1) *Austrolycichthys brachycephalus*.

Lycodes brachycephalus, Pappenheim, *Deutsche Südpolar-Exped.*, xiii., *Zool.*, v. p. 179, pl. x. fig. 3.

Depth of body 8 to 10½ in the length, length of head 5½ to 6⅔. Tail from less than 1½ to 1¼ as long as rest of fish. Diameter of eye 5 in the length of head. Maxillary extending to below anterior part of eye. About 90 rays in the dorsal fin, 70 in the anal, 10 in the caudal. Origin of dorsal above anterior part of pectoral, of anal

1⅔ to 1½ head-lengths behind head. Pectoral ⅔ or ¾ the length of head. Grayish or brownish.

Wilhelm Land, 380 metres.

Here described from two co-types, 155 and 150 mm. in total length. These differ greatly in form and proportions, as is shown by the accompanying figures, but I cannot doubt that they belong to the same species.

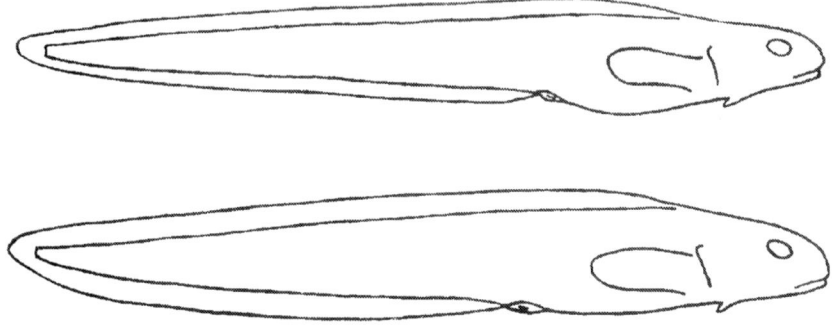

FIG. 2.—*Austrolycichthys brachycephalus.*

(2) *Austrolycichthys bothriocephalus.*

Lycodes bothriocephalus, Pappenheim, *Deutsche Südpolar-Exped.,* xiii., *Zool.,* v. p. 178, pl. x. fig. 2.

Apparently related to the preceding species, the more slender of the two examples of *A. brachycephalus* described above showing considerable resemblance to the photograph of the type. But this species is said to have more numerous fin-rays, about 110 in the dorsal and 90 in the anal.

Wilhelm Land, 380 metres.

Total length of the unique type, 181 mm.

6. *Austrolycus,* gen. nov.

Head depressed; body compressed posteriorly. Mouth subterminal, with short lateral cleft; teeth conical, uniserial on sides of jaws, bi- or tri-serial anteriorly; teeth on vomer in a group, on palatines in a single series. Gill-opening cleft downwards to middle of base of pectoral. Dorsal origin just behind head; pelvic fins present.

(1) *Austrolycus depressiceps,* sp. n. (Pl. V. fig. 1.)

Phucocœtes latitans (non Jenyns) Günth., *Cat. Fish.,* iv. p. 321 (1862); Smith, *Bihang Svensk. Vet.-Akad.,* xxiv., 1898, iv., No. 5, p. 51, pl. v. figs. 37-39; Garman, *Mem. Mus. Comp. Zool.,* xxiv., 1899, p. 138.

Depth of body about 10 in its length, length of head 5½ to 6½. Diameter of eye 6¼ to 9 in the length of head, much less than the interocular, but nearly equal to the interorbital width. Maxillary about reaching vertical from posterior margin of eye, 100 to 110 rays in the dorsal fin, 70 to 80 in the anal, 8 to 10 in the caudal, origin of dorsal above base of pectoral, of anal 1⅔ to 2 head-lengths behind head. Pectoral ⅔ the length of head. Brownish, abdomen pale; on side of head a sharp line between the dark brown above and pale yellow below, with the brown projecting downwards on the cheek as a bar; a pale transverse band across nape, another above end of pectoral extending on to dorsal fin, which may be followed by similar bands or spots.

Chile, Patagonia, Falkland Islands.

Here described from a large series of specimens measuring up to 250 mm in total length, including several obtained by the *Scotia* at Station 118, Port Stanley, Falkland Islands.

(2) *Austrolycus plates*.

Lycodes (Phucocœtes) plates, Steind., *Zool. Jahrb.*, Suppl. iv, p. 320, pl. xix, fig. 8 (1897–98).

Evidently closely related to the preceding species, differing in that the length of the head is ⅘ its distance from the vent, the tail is considerably longer than the head and trunk (only a little longer in *A. depressiceps*), and the coloration is different, the body being marked with broad cross bands, the interspaces between which correspond to the pale bands or spots on the back and dorsal fin of *A. depressiceps*.

Chile, Cape Espiritu Santo.

Total length 234 mm.

This may be the *Phucocœtes variegatus macropus* of Smitt (*Bihang Svensk. Vet.-Akad.*, xxiv, 1898, iv, No. 5, p. 44, pl. v, fig. 35).

7. *Phucocœtes*, Jenyns, 1842.[*]

Zool. "Beagle," Fish, p. 168 (1842).

Head and body compressed. Mouth subterminal; teeth conical, uniserial in upper jaw and on palatines, bi- or tri-serial in lower jaw; anterior pair of teeth in upper jaw, middle sometime tooth, and 1 or 2 pairs in lower jaw more or less enlarged and canine-like. Gill-opening small, above base of pectoral. Dorsal origin just behind head; pelvic fins present.

Phucocœtes latitans, Jenyns, *l. c.*, pl. xxix, fig. 3.

Lycodes davu, Boulenger, *Ann. Mag. Nat. Hist.* (7), vi, 1900, p. 53.

Depth of body 8 to 10 in the length, length of head 6½ to 7. Snout 1½ as long as diameter of eye, which is 6 to 7 in length of head, greater than interorbital width. Lower jaw included; maxillary extending to below posterior part of eye. Dorsal with

---

[*] Garman (*M. m. Mus. Comp. Zool.*, xxiv, 1899, p. 137) has described a fish from 16° N., 99° W., 660 fathoms, and has named it *Phucocœtes suspectus*. It is not a *Phucocœtes*, nor does it seem to be congeneric with any of the southern littoral forms.

about 100 rays, anal with about 80 caudal with 5 or 6. Origin of dorsal above base of pectoral, pectoral ⅔, pelvics ¼ as long as head. Brownish, upper half of head dark brown, with a pale yellow band from eye to shoulder; lower part of head pale yellowish.

Falkland Islands

Here described from two specimens 65 and 110 mm in total length, the latter the type of *L. flavus*. Four small examples were obtained by the *Scotia* at Station 118, Port Stanley, Falkland Islands.

8. *Crossolycus*, gen. nov.

Form elongate, compressed. Snout and lower jaw with fringes. Mouth subterminal, teeth in jaws conical, bi- or tri-serial, lower jaw with a posterior canine; palate toothless. Gill-opening almost entirely above base of pectoral. Dorsal origin above or a little in advance of base of pectoral; pelvic fins present.

(1) *Crossolycus chilensis* sp. n.

Lycodes (Iluocætes) fimbriatus (non Jenyns) Steind, *Zool Jahrb*, Suppl iv, 1898, p 322, pl xx fig 10

Depth of body equal to length of head, 6¾ in the length of the fish. Diameter of eye 7 in length of head and equal to interorbital width. Lips thick. Dorsal 80. Anal 60. Distance from head to origin of anal 1½ the length of head. Pectoral ⅔ as long as head. Head, body, and dorsal fin marbled with brown.

Chile, Cape Espiritu Santo

Steindachner's specimen measured 252 mm

(2) *Crossolycus fasciatus*

Iluocætes nmbriatus sub sp *fasciatus*, Lonnberg, *Swedish S Polar Exped*, *Fish*, p 20 (1905)

Depth of body 7½ in the length, length of head 5. Diameter of eye 5¾ in the length of head and equal to interorbital width. Distance from head to origin of anal 1½ the length of head. Pectoral a little more than ½ the length of head. Dark brown, with 5 or 6 whitish transverse bars.

Falkland Islands

Total length 74 mm

A specimen of 60 mm recorded by Lonnberg from Tierra del Fuego, uniform yellow in colour and differing somewhat in proportions, may belong to another species.

9. *Plateu*, Steind, 1897

Zool Jahrb, Suppl iv p 323

Teeth in jaws uniserial, incisor-like; palate toothless. Snout and lower jaw with fringes. Gill-opening cleft downwards to middle of base of pectoral. Dorsal origin above anterior part of pectoral. Pelvic fins present.

Platea insignis

Steind *l.c.*, pl. xx. fig. 12.

Depth of body 14½ in the length, length of head 7⅔. Dorsal with about 100 rays, anal with about 90. Body with dark spots and bars.

Chile, Cape Espiritu Santo.

Total length 265 mm.

10. *Maynea*, Cunningham, 1870.

Trans. Linn. Soc., xxvi. p. 471.
Gymnelichthys, Fischer, *Jahrb. Hamburg Wiss. Anst.*, ii, 1885, p. 60.

Elongate, compressed. Mouth terminal, teeth conical uniserial, in jaws and on vomer and palatines. Gill-opening cleft downwards to middle of base of pectoral. Dorsal origin just behind head. No pelvic fins.

(1) *Maynea patagonica*.

Cunningham, *l.c.*, p. 472; Günth., *Proc. Zool. Soc.*, 1881, p. 881, pl. ii. figs C and D.

Depth of body 10 or 11 in the length, length of head 6¾ to 7½. Diameter of eye 5 to 6 in length of head; interorbital region quite narrow. Maxillary extending to below anterior ¼ or middle of eye. About 120 rays in dorsal fin, 95 in anal, 8 in caudal. Origin of dorsal above base of pectoral, of anal 1⅖ to 1⅓ head-lengths behind head. Pectoral less than ½ as long as head. Yellowish, with broad brown crossbars separated by narrower interspaces.

Patagonia, Falkland Islands.

Here described from two specimens, the type from the Otter Islands 150 mm. in total length, and an example of 90 mm. from the Magellan Straits.

(2) *Maynea antarctica*.

Gymnelichthys antarcticus, Fischer, *Jahrb. Hamburg Wiss. Anst.*, ii, 1885 p. 61, pl. ii. fig. 9.

Maxillary extending to below posterior margin of eye. About 97 rays in the dorsal, 74 in the anal; origin of latter only 1⅓ head-lengths behind the head. No cross-bars.

South Georgia.

Total length 220 mm.

11. *Melanostigma*, Günth., 1881.

Proc. Zool. Soc., p. 21.

Compressed, elongate; skin loose, smooth, naked. Mouth terminal, oblique, teeth uniserial, in jaws and on vomer and palatines. Gill-opening small, above base of pectoral. Dorsal origin just behind head; no pelvic fins.

In addition to the species described below, this genus includes a few from deep waters of the North Atlantic and Pacific.

Melanostigma gelatinosum.

Günth., l.c.

Depth of body about 10 in the length, length of head 6. Diameter of eye 3½ in length of head, interorbital width about 12. Maxillary extending to below middle of eye. Distance from head to origin of anal equal to length of head; pectoral nearly ½ as long as head. Sides spotted and marbled with purplish grey; end of tail blackish; inside of mouth, gill-opening, and vent black.

Magellan Straits, 24 fathoms.

Here described from the type, a specimen of 140 mm.

III. A Monograph of the Nototheniiformes.

The division Nototheniiformes includes Percoids without pungent fin-spines, with the spinous dorsal, when developed, shorter than the long soft dorsal and anal, the

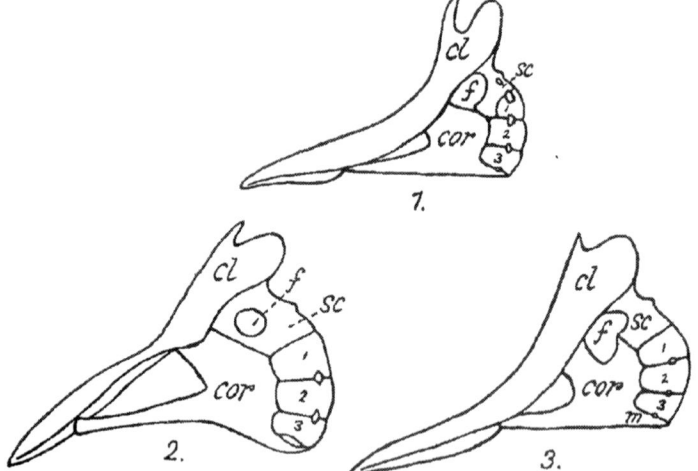

Fig. 3.—Pectoral fin-skeleton of 1, *Cottoperca gobio*; 2, *Trematomus newnesii*; and 3, *Notothenia coriiceps*. *cl*, cleithrum; *sc*, hypercoracoid (scapula); *f*, foramen; *cor*, hypocoracoid; *m*, metacoracoid process; 1, 2, 3, radials.

principal caudal rays reduced in number (usually 14), the pectorals typically broad-based and the pelvics jugular, separated by an interspace, and each formed of a spine and 5 branched rays. There is a single nostril on each side. The structure and position of the pectoral radials is highly characteristic; they are 3 in number, rather large flat plates; all or 2 are inserted on the hypocoracoid, and the lowest is the narrowest and has its lower edge in contact with the metacoracoid process. In other osteological characters the more generalised types are very similar to the Perciformes.

The group corresponds to the Nototheniidæ of BOULENGER and DOLLO, with the addition of *Pleuragramma*, which does not at all resemble *Leptoscopus* and after the exclusion of *Centropercis*, evidently related to *Champsodon*, and of *Acanthaphritis* (*Pteropsaron*), which is related to *Hemerocætes*. *Draconetta* is allied to the Callionymidæ, and its resemblances to *Harpagifer* are not due to affinity. As now restricted the Notothenniformes are characteristic of and peculiar to the Antarctic seas

FIG. 4.—Map showing the localities where Notothenniform fishes have been collected

and the region immediately to the north, ranging to S.E. Australia, New Zealand, Chile, Argentina, Tristan da Cunha, and St Paul Island.

There is every reason to suppose that the group has always been an Antarctic one, and seeing that it has become differentiated into four quite distinct families and into several genera, we may perhaps infer that there has been a large cold southern ocean throughout the greater part of the Tertiary period.

The group throws no light on the question of former extensions northward of the Antarctic Continent; at the present day there are littoral species common to Australia and New Zealand (*Bovichthys variegatus*) to New Zealand and South America (*Notothenia macrocephala, N. cornucola*), or to the Antarctic Continent and Kerguelen (*Notothenia coriiceps, Harpagifer bispinis*), and if under the existing conditions species may have this wide distribution, the fact that some are more restricted and are separated from the most nearly related forms by wide expanses of ocean can be explained without the theory of land-bridges.

Many of the more southern types appear to be circumpolar, for example, *Trematomus newnesi, T. borchgrevinki, T. bernacchii, T. hansoni, T. loennbergi, Pleuragramma antarcticum, Notothenia coriiceps*.

With the exception of *Pseudaphritis urvillii* from the rivers of Tasmania and S.E. Australia the Nototheniiform fishes are marine, and the great majority of them are littoral, several have been described as frequenting the rocks and weeds, but others prefer deeper water, the species varying in this respect like the Cottids and Gobies of our northern seas. Fishes pertaining to four genera (*Bathydraco, Gerlachea, Racovitzaia, Cryodraco*) live in the open sea, and probably at some distance below the surface.

Most of the fishes of this group feed on crustaceans, molluscs, etc (*cf* LONNBERG, *Fish Swedish South Polar Exped*, p 55), but *Gymnodraco* and the Chaenichthyidae are no doubt piscivorous. According to LONNBERG (*l c*, p 52) the breeding season varies, some species probably spawning in the spring, others in the summer, others in the autumn. The eggs are smaller in *Notothenia* and *Trematomus* than in *Artedidraco* and *Champsocephalus*, they are probably demersal in all, but certainly in the last two genera.

Synopsis of the Families

I. One radial on hypercoracoid, two on hypocoracoid, gill-membranes separate, free from isthmus, teeth on vomer and palatines, mouth protractile, snout not produced, a spinous dorsal fin   1 *Bovichthyidæ*

II. All three radials on hypocoracoid gill-membranes united free or attached to isthmus usually forming a fold across it, palate toothless

   A. Palatine and pterygoids normally developed
      Mouth protractile snout not produced, a spinous dorsal fin   2 *Nototheniidæ*
      Mouth not protractile snout produced, no spinous dorsal fin
           3 *Bathydraconidæ*

   B. Palatine in great part ligamentous, no mesopterygoid mouth not protractile, snout produced and depressed   4 *Chænichthyidæ*

Family 1 BOVICHTHYIDÆ

This family includes Nototheniiformes more generalised than the rest in the presence of bands of cardiform or villiform teeth not only in the jaws, but on the vomer and palatines, and in the separate free gill-membranes. All other members of the group have the palate toothless and the gill-membranes united, or joined to the isthmus. The snout is not produced, the mouth is protractile, the lateral line is complete and continuous, and a spinous dorsal fin is present. The skeleton is well ossified, there are 2 radials on the hypocoracoid and 1 on the hypercoracoid (fig. 3, 1), the palatine and pterygoids are normally developed. The vertebrae number 38 to 42 (13–16 + 22–29), præcaudals with parapophyses from the fifth or sixth, ribs and epipleurals on parapophyses, when these are developed.

Littoral fishes, with one species in fresh water.

Three genera.

1. *Pseudaphritis*, Casteln. 1872.

Proc. Zool. Soc. Victoria, i. p. 72; Ogilby, *Proc. Linn. Soc. N. S. Wales,* xxii, 1897 p. 559.

Body subcylindrical, fully scaled. Head small, scaly, somewhat depressed, narrowed forward, interorbital region flat. Teeth in bands in jaws and on vomer and palatines, lower jaw projecting. Operculum normal, with a weak spine, gill-membranes not united, free from isthmus. Origin of spinous dorsal at some distance behind head, rays of all the fins branched.

S.E. Australia and Tasmania: fresh-water.

Pseudaphritis urvillii.

Aphritis urvillii, Cuv. and Val., *Hist. Nat. Poiss.,* viii p. 484, pl. 243 (1831). Gunth. *Cat. Fish.,* ii p. 242 (1860).
Pseudaphritis bassii, Casteln., l. c.

Depth of body 5 to 6 in the length, length of head 3⅔ to 4. Diameter of eye 5½ to 7½ in the length of head, interorbital width 8 to 12. Maxillary extending to below eye; about 10 short gill-rakers on lower part of anterior arch. Dorsal VII–VIII, 19–20. Anal 23–25. 60 to 65 scales in the lateral line. Body marbled, dorsal and caudal spotted.

Rivers from New South Wales to South Australia and Tasmania.

Here described from eight specimens, 100 to 240 mm. in total length, from South Australia, Victoria, and Tasmania.

2. *Cottoperca*, Steind., 1876.

Sitzungsb. Akad. Wien, lxxii p. 66.

Head and body compressed, fully scaled. Head large, snout broad, interorbital region concave. Teeth in bands in jaws and on vomer and palatines, lower jaw somewhat the shorter. Operculum normal, with a weak spine, gill-membranes not united, free from isthmus. Spinous dorsal originating above operculum; rays of soft dorsal and anal unbranched, lower pectoral rays simple, more or less thickened and partly free distally.

Patagonia, Magellan Straits, Falkland Islands.

(1) *Cottoperca gobio* (Pl IV fig 3.)

Aphritis gobio, Gunth, Ann Mag Nat Hist (3), vii, 1861, p 88, and "*Challenger*" Shore Fish p 21, pl ix (1880)
Cottoperca rosenbergii, Steind Sitzungsb Akad Wien, lxxii, 1876, p 67, pl v fig 1

Depth of body about 4 in the length, length of head about 2¼. Diameter of eye 4 to 8 in the length of head, interorbital width 13 to 16. Maxillary extending to below posterior part or posterior edge of eye, 5 or 6 short gill-rakers on lower part of anterior arch. Dorsal (VI) VII, 22–23. Anal 20–23. Dorsal spines and rays increasing in length with age, the longest varying from ⅓ to ¾ the length of head. Pectoral about ½ the length of head, six lowest rays simple, somewhat thickened. Caudal subtruncate. Least depth of caudal peduncle greater than the diameter of eye, except in quite young specimens. About 60 scales in a lateral longitudinal series, or 65 in the lateral line, which is complete and continuous. Orange-yellow, with three broad brownish cross-bars on upper part of body; head and sides of body spotted and marbled with brown.

Patagonia; Tierra del Fuego, Falkland Islands.

Here described from nine specimens, 130 to 480 mm in total length, from Magellan and the Falklands, at depths varying from 6 to 147 fathoms, including the types of the species and a specimen from Station 349, Port William, Falkland Islands, taken by the *Scotia* in January 1903.

(2) *Cottoperca macrophthalma*, sp n (Pls IV fig 2, and V fig 2.)

Depth of body 4 to 5 in the length, length of head (to opercular spine) 2⅔ to 2⅔. Diameter of eye 3½ to 5 in the length of head, interorbital width 13 to 16. Maxillary extending to below posterior part or margin of eye, or a little beyond. 5 to 7 short gill-rakers on lower part of anterior arch. Dorsal VII (VIII), 21–24. Anal 20–22. In the young first dorsal spine longest, ⅓ the length of head and as long as soft rays; in the adult, fourth or fifth spine longest, sometimes ½ the length of head, longest soft rays sometimes ¼ the length of head. Other fins, scales, coloration, etc, as in *C gobio*. Least depth of caudal peduncle not more than diameter of eye.

Ten specimens from Station 346, the Burdwood Bank south of the Falkland Islands, 54° 25′ S, 57° 32′ W, taken by the *Scotia* in 56 fathoms on 1st December 1903, and three from Magellan Straits, 100 to 450 mm in total length.

(3) *Cottoperca macrocephala*
Roule, Bull Mus Paris, 1911, p 277 (1912)

Eye large. Head longer and fins lower than in *C macrophthalma*. Seven simple pectoral rays. Patagonia.

3. *Bovichthys*, Cuv. and Val., 1831.

Hist. Nat. Poiss., viii. p. 486.

Differs from *Cottoperca* in the naked head and body, the abnormal operculum, which has a very strong spine and a superior process which articulates with the post-temporal, and in the enlarged and partly free posterior anal rays.

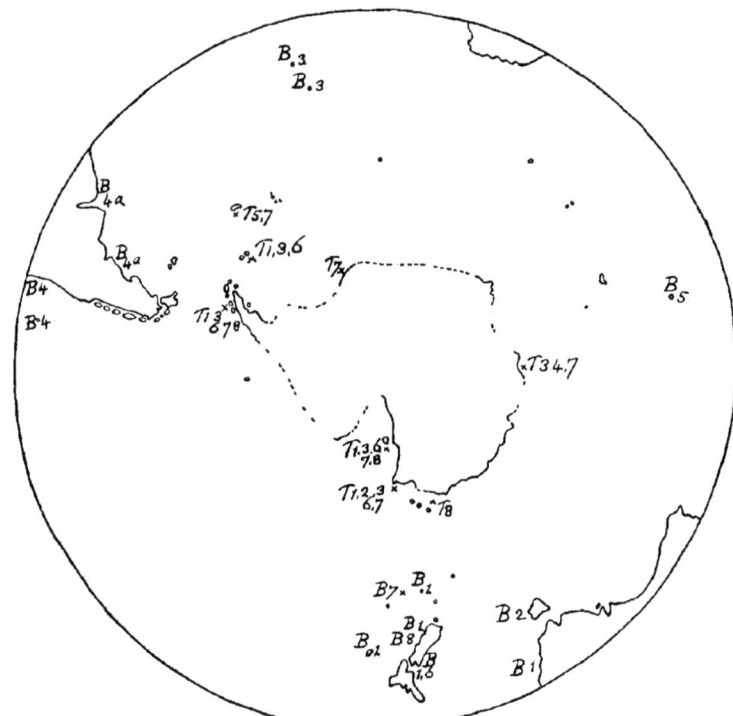

Fig. 5.—Distribution of *Bovichthys* and *Trematomus*, respectively the northernmost and southernmost Nototheniform genera.

B = *Bovichthys*. 1, *B. variegatus*; 2, *B. angustifrons*; 3, *B. diacanthus*; 4, *B. chilensis*; 4a, *B.* sp.; 5, *B. veneris*; 6, *B. decipiens*; 7, *B. psychrolutes*; 8, *B. roseopictus*.
T = *Trematomus*. 1, *T. newnesi*; 2, *T. nicolai*; 3, *T. borchgrevinki*; 4, *T. brachysoma*; 5, *T. vicarius*; 6, *T. bernacchii*; 7, *T. hansoni*; 8, *T. loennbergii*.

Note that in *Bovichthys* none, in *Trematomus* most, of the species appear to be circumpolar.

Chile, Argentina, Tristan da Cunha and Gough Island, St. Paul, S.E. Australia and Tasmania, New Zealand and neighbouring islands.

Synopsis of the Species

I Interorbital region distinctly concave
    Interorbital width $\frac{1}{10}$, pectoral fin $\frac{3}{4}$ the length of head   1 *variegatus*
    Interorbital width $\frac{1}{12}$ or $\frac{1}{13}$, pectoral fin $\frac{2}{3}$ the length of head   2 *angustifrons*.
    Interorbital width $\frac{1}{11}$, pectoral fin $\frac{4}{5}$ the length of head   3 *diacanthus*
II Interorbital region nearly flat
    Interorbital width $\frac{1}{8}$ the length of head, pectoral fin $\frac{2}{3}$ 4 *chilensis*
    Interorbital width more than $\frac{1}{2}$ the diameter of eye, which is $\frac{1}{4}$ the length of head, pectoral extending to vent   .   5 *veneris*
    Interorbital width $6\frac{1}{2}$ in length of head, pectoral extending well beyond origin of anal   6 *decipiens*
    Interorbital width 5 in length of head   7 *psychrolutes*
    Interorbital width $3\frac{1}{3}$ in length of head   8 *roseopictus*

(1) *Bovichthys variegatus*

Richards, "*Erebus*" and "*Terror*' *Fish*, p 56, pl xxxiv figs 1-4 (1846), Gunth, *Cat Fish*, ii p 250 (1860)

Depth of body 4 to 5 in the length, length of head $2\frac{1}{4}$ to 3 Diameter of eye 4 to $4\frac{1}{2}$ in the length of head, interorbital width 10 Interorbital region moderately concave, maxillary extending to below anterior $\frac{1}{3}$ of eye, opercular spine equal to or less than diameter of eye, 8 gill-rakers on lower part of anterior arch Dorsal VII–VIII, 18–20. Anal 14–15 Pectoral $\frac{3}{4}$ the length of head Caudal subtruncate Caudal peduncle longer than deep Body with irregular dark cross-bars and usually with pale spots and vermiculations, spinous dorsal marbled, sometimes with a blackish blotch posteriorly, soft dorsal, caudal, and pectoral with series of dark spots, anal with a dark longitudinal band

S E Australia, New Zealand and neighbouring islands

Here described from six specimens, 75 to 200 mm in total length, including the types of the species, from New South Wales (*Haslar*), New Zealand (*Otago Mus*, *Hutton*), and Campbell Island (*Southern Cross*)

(2) *Bovichthys angustifrons*, sp n (Pl IV fig 1)

Depth of body $4\frac{2}{3}$ to 5 in the length, length of head $2\frac{3}{5}$ to $2\frac{3}{4}$ Diameter of eye 4 in the length of head, interorbital width 12 or 13 Interorbital region moderately concave, maxillary extending to below anterior $\frac{1}{3}$ of eye, opercular spine nearly as long as diameter of eye; 8 gill-rakers on lower part of anterior arch Dorsal VIII, 19 Anal 14 Pectoral $\frac{2}{3}$ the length of head Caudal subtruncate Caudal peduncle longer than deep Dark spots on the head and blotches or bars on the body, soft dorsal and caudal with series of spots on the rays

Here described from two specimens, 160 and 115 mm in total length the former from Tasmania (*Allport*) the latter without locality (*Chatham Museum*)

(3) *Borichthys diacanthus* (Pl IX fig 5)

Callionymus diacanthus, Carmich., Trans Linn Soc, xii, 1818, p 501, pl xxvi
Borichthys diacanthus, Gunth, Cat Fish, ii p 249 (1860)

Depth of body 5 in the length, length of head 3. Diameter of eye $4\frac{1}{2}$ in the length of head, interorbital width 11. Interorbital region concave, maxillary extending to below anterior $\frac{1}{4}$ of eye, opercular spine $\frac{2}{3}$ the diameter of eye, 9 gill-rakers on lower part of anterior arch. Dorsal VIII 20. Anal 15. Pectoral $\frac{3}{5}$ the length of head. Caudal subtruncate. Caudal peduncle longer than deep.

Tristan da Cunha, Gough Island

Here described from a specimen of 120 mm obtained by the *Scotia* at Gough Island, shore

The species was originally described from Tristan da Cunha, where it is said to be very common among the rocks and to attain a length of 7 inches. CARMICHAEL describes the colour as olive, with green blotches and white dots

(4) *Borichthys chilensis*, sp n

Borichthys diacanthus (non Carmichael), Cuv and Val, Hist Nat Poiss, viii p 487, pl 244
(1831), Steind, Zool Jahrb, Suppl iv, 1897-8, p 300, pl xx fig 1

Depth of body 5 in the length, length of head 3 to $3\frac{1}{4}$. Diameter of eye $4\frac{1}{4}$ to $4\frac{1}{2}$ in the length of head, interorbital width 9. Interorbital space nearly flat, maxillary extending to below anterior $\frac{1}{3}$ of eye, opercular spine as long as or shorter than eye. 8 gill-rakers on lower part of anterior arch. Dorsal VIII, 21. Anal 14-16. Pectoral $\frac{2}{3}$ the length of head. Caudal truncate. Caudal peduncle longer than deep. Body marbled, spinous dorsal dusky, with a dark blotch posteriorly, soft dorsal with 2 or 3 series of dark spots, caudal dusky with orange posterior margin, lower fins orange more or less spotted

Chile, Juan Fernandez

Here described from two specimens from Chile (*Delfin*), 92 and 96 mm in total length

BERG (Ann Mus Buenos Aires, ii 1897, p 298) has recorded a species of *Borichthys* from Argentina as *Borichthys diacanthus*. This may prove to be *B chilensis*, more probably it is a new species as yet undescribed

(5) *Borichthys renerts*

Borichthys psycurolutes (non Gunth.), Kner, Novara Fische, p 128, pl vi (1860)
" *renerts*, Sauvage, Arch Zool exp, viii, 1879, p 25

Depth of body 5 in the length, length of head about $3\frac{1}{4}$. Diameter of eye 4 in the length of head. Interorbital region only slightly concave, its width rather more than $\frac{1}{2}$ the diameter of eye. Maxillary extending to below anterior $\frac{1}{3}$ of eye, opercular spine $\frac{2}{3}$ the diameter of eye Dorsal VIII, 19–20 Anal 14-15 Pectoral $\frac{4}{5}$ or $\frac{5}{6}$ the length of head Caudal rounded or subtruncate Caudal peduncle longer than deep

Island of St Paul

KNER'S and SAUVAGE'S descriptions are based on specimens of 9 or 10 inches

(6) *Bovichthys decipiens*, sp. n (Pl IX fig 1)

Depth of body 4 in the length, length of head $2\frac{3}{4}$ Diameter of eye $3\frac{1}{2}$ in the length of head, interorbital width $6\frac{1}{2}$ Interorbital space nearly flat, maxillary extending to below anterior $\frac{1}{3}$ of eye, opercular spine a little shorter than eye, 8 gill-rakers on lower part of anterior arch Dorsal VIII, 19 Anal 14 Pectoral $\frac{4}{5}$ the length of head Caudal peduncle longer than deep Body with cross-bars, spinous dorsal with a blotch posteriorly, dorsal and pectoral with series of spots, caudal barred

A specimen of 41 mm from Cook's Straits (*Hector*) is very similar in appearance to *B variegatus*

(7) *Bovichthys psychrolutes*

Gunth, *Cat Fish*, ii p 250 (1860)

Depth of body 4 in the length, length of head 3 Diameter of eye $3\frac{1}{2}$ in the length of head, interorbital width 5 Interorbital region nearly flat, maxillary extending to below anterior $\frac{1}{3}$ of eye, opercular spine as long as eye 8 gill-rakers on lower part of anterior arch Dorsal VIII, 20 Anal 14 Pectoral $\frac{4}{5}$ the length of head Caudal subtruncate Caudal peduncle longer than deep Bluish-olive, fins pale

Here described from the type, a specimen 38 mm. in total length, from S W of the Antipodes Islands (50° S, 170° W)

(8) *Bovichthys roseopictus*

Hutton, *Trans N Zeal Inst*, xxxvi, 1903, art ix

Depth of body $5\frac{1}{2}$, length of head $4\frac{1}{2}$ in total length Diameter of eye 3 in length of head, interorbital width $3\frac{1}{3}$ Top of head smooth, with two small ridges Dorsal VIII, 18 (?) Anal 13 (?) Pectoral as long as head Caudal apparently truncated Back dark olivaceous brown, sides and abdomen silvery, a pink spot at base of operculum and 5 bright rose-pink bands on each side

New Zealand, known from a single specimen of 46 mm picked up on the beach at Sumner, Canterbury

Family 2 NOTOTHENIIDÆ

Differ from the Bovichthyidæ in the toothless palate, the united gill-membranes, and in having all 3 radials on the hypocoracoid (fig 3, 2 and 3) Vertebræ 45–56 (16–20 + 25–35)

In the typical genera the skeleton is well ossified, and the rather strong ribs and epipleurals are inserted on well-developed parapophyses, or only the first one or two are sessile. In *Pleuragramma* the skeleton is weak, with the bones thin and papery, the vertebral centra are thin cylinders of bone, parapophyses are developed on the posterior præcaudals only, and the ribs and epipleurals are feeble.

Synopsis of the Genera

I. Body scaly, gill-membranes forming a fold across the isthmus; opercles normal.
  A. Hypercoracoid enclosing its foramen.
    Lateral line scales with tubules or pits   1. *Trematomus*
    Lateral line scales merely notched   2. *Pleuragramma*
  B. Foramen partly bordered by hypocoracoid.
    1. Two or three lateral lines; maxillary usually extending to below eye; pectoral rounded or vertically truncated.
      Teeth in bands   3. *Notothenia*
      Teeth uniserial   4. *Dissostichus*
    2. One lateral line; maxillary not reaching eye in the adult fish; pectoral very obliquely truncated, the upper rays longest   5. *Eleginops*
II. Body naked, gill-membranes broadly united to isthmus, operculum hooked upwards posteriorly, its upper edge deeply concave; foramen partly bordered by hypocoracoid.
  A mental barbel, opercles not spinate   6. *Artedidraco*
  No barbel, operculum and subopercnlum each forming a strong spine   7. *Harpagifer*

1. *Trematomus*, Bouleng., 1902

"*Southern Cross*" *Pisces*, p. 177

Body scaly; 2 lateral lines with tubular or pitted scales. Mouth moderate or rather large; jaws with bands of villiform teeth. Gill-membranes united, free or forming a free fold across isthmus. Skeleton well ossified; vertebræ 52–56 (17–21 + 32–35), most of the præcaudals with parapophyses to which the ribs and epipleurals are attached; hypercoracoid enclosing its foramen (fig. 3, 2). A spinous dorsal fin; pectoral rounded or sub-vertically truncated.

Coasts of the Antarctic Continent; South Orkneys and South Georgia (fig. 5, p. 254).

The difference between *Notothenia*, with the hypocoracoid bordering the foramen, and *Trematomus*, with the foramen enclosed in the hypercoracoid, may not be very important, and PAPPENHEIM believed that he found both conditions in one species (*Deutsche Südpolar-Exped.*, XIII., *Zool.*, v. p. 166, figs.), but this seems to have been an error, the specimen with perforate hypercoracoid being *Trematomus hansoni* and not *Notothenia lepidorhinus*. PAPPENHEIM (*l.c.*, p. 170) states that *T. bernacchii* is a *Notothenia* in the structure of its pectoral arch; I have examined a large series of specimens, and find that the hypercoracoid encloses its foramen in all.

Synopsis of the Species.

I Upper surface of head naked
  A Cheeks and opercles fully scaled
    Interorbital width $3\frac{1}{3}$ to 5 in length of head   D VI–VIII, 32–38
    A 32–36   1 *newnesii*
    Interorbital width 8 or 9 in length of head   D IV, 37   A 32–33
         2 *nicolai*
  B Cheeks and opercles scaly above, naked below, interorbital width 3 to $5\frac{1}{2}$ in length of head
    D V–VI, 34–37   A 31–33   3 *borchgrevinki*
    D IV–V, 30–33   A 29–30   4 *brachysoma*

II Occiput scaly
  A Interorbital region naked, or not fully scaled   D IV–VI, 33–38   A 31–35
    Diameter of eye $4\frac{2}{5}$ in length of head, interorbital width about 5 (in a specimen of about 270 mm), 55 to 59 scales in a longitudinal series   5 *vicarius*
    Diameter of eye 3 to $4\frac{1}{3}$ in length of head, interorbital width 5 to 9 (in specimens up to 340 mm), 60 to 75 scales in a longitudinal series   6 *bernacchii*
  B Interorbital region fully scaled, width 5 to 10 in length of head
    D V–VII, 36–41   A 33–36   . 7 *hansoni*
    D V–VI, 33–34   A 31–33   8. *loennbergii*

(1) *Trematomus newnesii*

Bouleng., "*Southern Cross*" *Pisces*, p 177, pl xi (1902)
Notothenia cyaneobrancha, Vaill., *Exped Antarct Française, Poiss*, p 26 (1906)
   "   *microlepidota*, Vaill., *t c*, p 35
   "   *hodgsoni*, Bouleng., *Nat Antarctic Exped, Nat Hist*, ii, *Fish*, p 2, pl i fig 2 (1907)

Depth of body 4 to $5\frac{1}{2}$ in the length, length of head $3\frac{1}{4}$ to $4\frac{1}{4}$ Diameter of eye 3 to $4\frac{1}{3}$ in the length of head, interorbital width $3\frac{1}{3}$ to 5 Maxillary extending to below anterior part or middle of eye (young) or beyond (adult), upper surface of head naked, cheeks and opercles scaly, 15 to 20 gill-rakers on lower part of anterior arch Dorsal VI–VIII, 32–38 Anal 32–36 Pectoral $\frac{3}{4}$ the length of head or more, longer than pelvics, which reach the vent in the young, but not in the adult Caudal truncate Caudal peduncle about as long as deep 68 to 86 scales in a longitudinal series from above base of pectoral fin to caudal, 40 to 52 in upper lateral line, which ends below posterior rays of dorsal, 3 to 19 in lower lateral line Brownish, usually spotted or marbled or with irregular cross-bars, spinous dorsal blackish, other fins dusky, often with small dark spots

Here described from a large series of specimens, 50 to 200 mm in total length, including the types of the species and of *N hodgsoni* The types came from Duke of

York Island, near Cape Adare, 3 to 5 fathoms, and Cape Adare, 4 to 8 fathoms, those of *N. hodgsoni* from the *Discovery* winter quarters, Ross Island. The *Scotia* specimens are all from Station 325, Scotia Bay, South Orkneys; others in the British Museum are from the South Shetlands.

(2) *Trematomus nicolai*

Notothenia nicolai, Boulenger, 'Southern Cross' Pisces, p. 184, pl. xv (1902).

Depth of body nearly 4 in the length, length of head $3\frac{1}{3}$ to $3\frac{1}{2}$. Diameter of eye 3 to $3\frac{1}{3}$ in the length of head, interorbital width 8 to 9. Maxillary extending to below anterior $\frac{1}{4}$ or $\frac{1}{3}$ of eye; upper surface of head naked; cheeks and opercles scaly; 11 or 12 gill-rakers on lower part of anterior arch. Dorsal IV, 37. Anal 32-33. Pectoral $\frac{2}{3}$ to $\frac{3}{4}$ length of head, somewhat longer than pelvics, which reach vent or origin of anal. Caudal rounded. Caudal peduncle nearly as long as deep. 58 to 62 scales in a longitudinal series from above base of pectoral fin to caudal; 39 to 43 in upper lateral line, which ends below posterior rays of dorsal, 8 to 18 in lower lateral line. Brownish, with dark cross-bars and sometimes with small dark spots; fins dusky. Victoria Land.

Here described from the types, three specimens 150 to 250 mm. in total length, from Cape Adare, 5 to 8 fathoms, and Duke of York Island, near Cape Adare, 4 fathoms.

The pectoral arch of this species is exactly similar to that of the closely related *T. newnesi*, as figured on p. 249.

(3) *Trematomus borchgrevinki*

Boulenger, 'Southern Cross' Pisces, p. 179, pl. xii (1902). Pappenheim, *Deutsche Südpolar-Exped.*, xiii, *Zool.*, v, p. 171 (1912).

Depth of body 4 to 5 in the length, length of head $3\frac{1}{2}$ to $4\frac{1}{4}$. Diameter of eye 4 to 5 in length of head, interorbital width 3 to 4. Maxillary extending to below anterior $\frac{1}{3}$ of eye; upper surface of head naked; upper parts of cheeks and opercles scaly; 16 to 19 gill-rakers on lower part of anterior arch. Dorsal V-VI, 34-37. Anal 31-33. Pectoral $\frac{1}{2}$ to $\frac{5}{8}$ the length of head, longer than pelvics, which rarely reach the vent. Caudal rounded or subtruncate. Caudal peduncle as long as deep, or deeper than long. 78 to 96 scales in a longitudinal series from above base of pectoral fin to caudal; lateral lines vestigial, without or with only a few tubules. Yellowish, with dark spots or irregular cross-bars; dorsal and caudal sometimes with series of spots.

Graham Land and neighbouring islands; Wilhelm Land; Victoria Land.

Here described from several specimens, 180 to 270 mm. in total length, including the types of the species, from Cape Adare and Duke of York Island, near Cape Adare (*Southern Cross*), and examples from the *Discovery* winter quarters, Ross Island. A specimen of 80 mm. was obtained in March 1903 by the *Scotia*, at Station 325, in Scotia Bay, South Orkneys, depth 10 to 15 fathoms.

(4) *Trematomus brachysoma*.

Pappenheim, *Deutsche Südpolar-Exped.*, xiii., *Zool.*, v. p. 172 (1912).

Depth of body $4\frac{1}{10}$ to $4\frac{7}{8}$ in the length, length of head 3 to $3\frac{2}{3}$. Diameter of eye $3\frac{2}{3}$ to $3\frac{3}{4}$ in the length of head, interorbital width 4 to $5\frac{1}{2}$. Maxillary extending to below anterior part or middle of eye; upper surface of head naked; upper parts of cheeks and opercles scaly; 16 to 19 gill-rakers on lower part of anterior arch. Dorsal IV–V, 30–33. Anal 26–30. Caudal rounded. Caudal peduncle a little deeper than long. 65 to 75 scales in a longitudinal series. Yellowish brown; head and back dark; a series of 6 dark spots from operculum to caudal, and 5 below them at level of base of pectoral; a dark spot at tip of spinous dorsal; soft dorsal with irregular dark cross-bars.

Wilhelm Land.

Total length 93 to 166 mm.

(5) *Trematomus vicarius*.

Trematomus bernacchii subsp. *vicarius*, Lönnberg, *Swedish South Polar Exped.*, Fish., p. 26 (1905).
? *Notothenia dubia*, Lönnberg, *l.c.*, p. 28, pl. iii. fig. 9.

Depth of body $3\frac{1}{2}$ in the length, length of head $3\frac{1}{2}$. Diameter of eye $4\frac{3}{4}$ in length of head, interorbital width about 5. Maxillary extending to below anterior $\frac{1}{3}$ of eye;

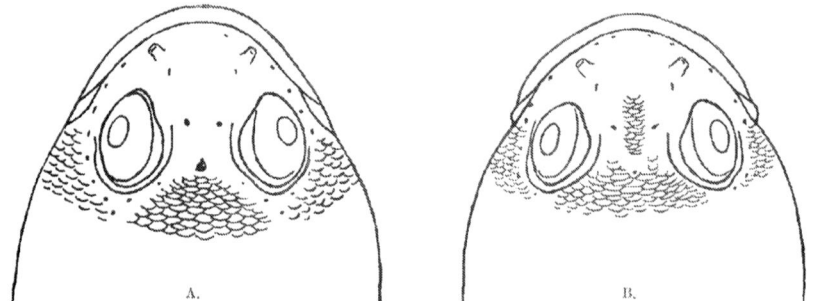

Fig. 6.—Head seen from above of A, *Trematomus bernacchii*, and B, *T. vicarius*.

cheeks, opercles, and occiput scaly; anterior part of interorbital region scaly in the middle; about 12 gill-rakers on lower part of anterior arch. Dorsal V, 33. Anal 31. Pectorals $\frac{3}{4}$, pelvics $\frac{1}{2}$ the length of head. Caudal rounded. Caudal peduncle much deeper than long. 56 to 59 scales in a longitudinal series, 34 in upper lateral line; lower lateral line without tubules.

South Georgia.

Lönnberg's description is based on a single specimen, 240 mm. in length to base of caudal fin.

Dr Lönnberg has kindly sent me a sketch of the upper surface of the head of the type, which is here reproduced, together with a figure of the head of a specimen of

T. bernacchii of the same size. After comparing the type with examples of *T. bernacchii* that I sent him, Dr. Lönnberg writes that the caudal peduncle is notably deeper and that the scales are larger.

Dr. Lönnberg has also sent me one of the types of *N. dubia* for examination. The specimen is 50 mm. in total length, and is a *Trematomus* with the head scaled as in *T. bernacchii*, but with a smaller eye (3⅔ in the length of head) and broader interorbital region (6½ in the length of head) than young examples of that species. I count Dorsal V, 37; Anal 32; 55 scales in a longitudinal series, 30 in the lateral line; 13 gill-rakers on the lower part of anterior arch. It seems probable that this may be a young example of *T. vicarius*, although the interorbital region is sealeless.

(6) *Trematomus bernacchii*

Boulenger, "*Southern Cross*" *Pisces*, p. 181, pl. xiv (1902).
Notothenia elegans, Vaill., *Expéd. Antarct. Française, Poiss.*, p. 28 (1906).

Depth of body 3 to 4½ in the length, length of head 3½ to 4. Diameter of eye 3 to 4⅓ in the length of head, interorbital width 5 to 9. Maxillary extending to below anterior part or middle of eye; occiput, cheeks, and opercles scaly; interorbital region naked or with a median series of scales; 13 to 15 gill-rakers on lower part of anterior arch. Dorsal IV–VI, 34–38. Anal 31–35. Pectoral about ⅔ the length of head; pelvics just reaching anal in young, but not in adult. Caudal rounded. Caudal peduncle deeper than long. 60 to 75 scales in a longitudinal series from above base of pectoral fin to caudal; 30 to 42 in upper lateral line; lower lateral line usually without tubules. Large dark spots in 2 or 3 alternating series; upper ½ of spinous dorsal blackish.

Graham Land and neighbouring islands; Victoria Land.

Here described from several specimens, 90 to 340 mm. in total length including the types of the species from Cape Adare, 5 to 8 fathoms, and Duke of York Island, near Cape Adare, 3 to 4 fathoms (*Southern Cross*); examples from the *Discovery* winter quarters, Ross Island, and two from Station 325, Scotia Bay, South Orkneys, collected by the *Scotia*.

In this species the interorbital region seems to be always sealeless in the young, and is often so in the adult fish.

(7) *Trematomus hansoni*

Boulenger, "*Southern Cross*" *Pisces*, p. 180, pl. xiii (1902).
Trematomus hansoni subsp. *georgianus*, Lönnberg, *Swedish South Polar Exped., Fish.*, p. 25, pl. v. fig. 17 (1905).
Notothenia sima, Vaill., *Exped. Antarct. Française, Poiss.*, p. 23 (1906).
 „ *lepidorhinus* (part), Pappenheim, *Deutsche Sudpolar Exped.*, xiii., *Zool.*, v. p. 169 (1912).

Depth of body 3½ to 4⅔ in the length, length of head 3¼ to 4. Diameter of eye 3¾ to 5 in the length of head, interorbital width 5 to 6½. Maxillary extending to below anterior part of middle of eye, occiput, interorbital region, cheeks, and opercles scaly, 13 to 16 gill-rakers on lower part of anterior arch. Dorsal V–VII, 36–41. Anal 33–36. Pectoral ⅓ to ⅖ the length of head, longer than pelvics which do not reach the vent. Caudal subtruncate. Caudal peduncle about as long as deep. 60 to 68 scales in a longitudinal series from above base of pectoral fin to caudal, 38 to 46 in upper lateral line, lower lateral line usually without tubules. Brownish, with large dark spots or cross-bars, head often spotted, fins usually barred with series of dark spots.

South Georgia, Graham Land, Coats Land, Wilhelm Land, Victoria Land.

Here described from several specimens, 160 to 380 mm. in total length, including the types of the species, from Cape Adare, 4 to 8 fathoms, and Duke of York Island, near Cape Adare, 3 to 4 fathoms (*Southern Cross*), examples from the *Discovery* winter quarters, Ross Island, and three from Coats Land, Station 411, 74° 01′ S., 22° 00′ W., 161 fathoms, temperature 28.9° F., trap, March 1904.

Dr LÖNNBERG's supposed subspecies from South Georgia is fully identical with the typical form. He gives the number of anal rays as (31) 32–33, but the figure shows 36, and in an example that he has kindly sent me I count 35. There is no difference in the shape of the pectoral.

Dr PAPPENHEIM has kindly sent me for examination the smallest specimen of his *N. lepidorhinus*, 160 mm. in total length, which he has noticed as differing from the types in the larger number of dorsal rays (38 instead of 32 or 33). It differs also in the naked snout and præorbital, shorter pelvic fins, lower lateral line without tubules, foramen enclosed in the hypercoracoid, etc., and is in every way similar to one of the types of *T. hansoni*, with which I have compared it.

(8) *Trematomus loennbergii*, sp. n. (Pl VIII fig 4.)

Depth of body 4⅔ to 5 in length, length of head 3 to 3¼. Diameter of eye 3 to 4¼ in the length of head, interorbital width 7 to 10. Maxillary extending to below anterior ¼ of eye, upper surface of head to nostrils, cheeks, and opercles scaly, 13 gill-rakers on lower part of anterior arch. Dorsal V–VI, 33–34. Anal 31–33. Pectoral as long as or a little shorter than head, pelvics extending to origin of anal or beyond. Caudal rounded. Caudal peduncle longer than deep. 60 to 70 scales in a longitudinal series from above pectoral fin to caudal, 36 to 42 in upper lateral line, which ends below posterior rays of dorsal, lower lateral line without tubules.

Victoria Land, Graham Land, and neighbouring islands.

Here described from three specimens, two from the *Discovery* collection—the larger, 132 mm. in total length, from south-west of the Balleny Islands, 254 fathoms, the smaller, 65 mm., in total length, from Tent Island, near Ross Island. The third example, also about 65 mm., is from Seymour Island, and has been sent to me for examination by Dr LÖNNBERG, who has recorded this species as *Notothenia nicolai*

(*Swedish South Polar Exped. Fish*, p. 45). I have named the species after Dr. Lönnberg in recognition of his kindness in sending me this and other specimens.

2. Pleuragramma, Bouleng., 1902.

"*Southern Cross*" *Pisces*, p. 187 (1902).

Closely related to *Trematomus*, differing especially in the very thin cycloid scales, the absence of pitted or tubular lateral line scales, and the feebly ossified skeleton, with parapophyses developed only on the posterior præcaudal vertebræ.

Coasts of the Antarctic Continent.

Boulenger has placed this genus in the family Leptoscopidæ, but it has no affinity with *Leptoscopus* and, on the other hand, is very near to *Trematomus*. A comparison of *Pleuragramma antarcticum* with *Trematomus newnesi* shows a very close agreement in external and internal characters, even to the number of fin-rays and vertebræ; the pectoral arch is precisely similar. In *Pleuragramma* the two lateral lines are marked by scales with notched posterior edges, or, if the scales have been lost, by series of pores.

Pleuragramma antarcticum.

Bouleng., *l.c.*, p. xviii. Vaillant, *Exped. Antarct. Française, Poiss.*, p. 18 (1906). Pappenheim *Deutsche Südpolar Exped.*, xiii, *Zool.*, v. p. 164.

Depth of body 5 to 6 in the length; length of head $3\frac{1}{4}$ to 4. Diameter of eye $3\frac{1}{4}$ to $3\frac{3}{4}$ in the length of head; interorbital width 5 to 6. Lower jaw projecting; maxillary extending to below anterior $\frac{1}{3}$ of eye; upper surface of head naked; cheeks and opercles scaly; 20 to 25 gill rakers on lower part of anterior arch. Dorsal VI–VII 34–37. Anal 36–38. Pectoral truncated, $\frac{1}{2}$ to $\frac{3}{5}$ length of head. Caudal slightly emarginate. About 55 scales in a lateral longitudinal series. Silvery, back darker; sides and back powdered with blackish dots.

Graham Land, Wilhelm Land, Victoria Land.

Here described from several specimens, 150 to 200 mm. in total length, including the types of the species from Victoria Land (*Southern Cross*) and examples from near Cape Armitage, Ross Island, and from south-west of the Balleny Islands (*Discovery*). Vaillant gives D. V, 39; A. 38; Sq. 44, for specimens from Graham Land, and Pappenheim, D. V–VIII, 34–38; A. 36–38; Sq. 56–60, for examples from Wilhelm Land.

3. Notothenia, Richards, 1844.

"*Erebus*' and '*Terror*" *Fish*, p. 5. Günth., *Cat. Fish.*, ii. p. 260 (1860).
Macronotothen, Gill, *Proc. Acad. Philad.*, 1861, p. 521.

Differs from *Trematomus* only in that the hypercoracoid foramen is margined below by the hypocoracoid (fig. 3, 3, p. 249).

Coasts of the Antarctic Continent and northwards to Patagonia, the Falkland

Islands, South Sandwich Islands, Marion Islands, Kerguelen, southern New Zealand, and Chatham Islands.

Although the interorbital region is relatively broader in the larger fish its width, compared with the length of the head, is an important specific character. By the "interorbital width" is here understood the actual width of the osseous interorbital space; this is nearly always less, and when narrow proportionately much less, than the interorbital width as measured by BOULENGER.

Synopsis of the Species

I. Opercles fully scaled.
    A. Upper surface and sides of head scaly, except snout and præorbital; interorbital width ⅕ the length of head or more.
        1. Upper lateral line of 62 to 65 tubular scales, D VI, 32–34 A 30–32
    3 lateral lines   1 *trigramma*
    2 lateral lines   2 *canina*
        2. Upper lateral line of 40 to 55 tubular scales. D V–VII, 32–37 A 31–35
            a 21 to 25 gill rakers on lower part of anterior arch. D VII (VIII) 34–36 A 32–34   3 *ramsayi*
            b 14 to 19 gill-rakers on lower part of anterior arch.
                α Upper lateral line not or scarcely extending beyond end of dorsal fin; diameter of eye 4¼ to 6 in length of head (in specimens up to 250 mm.) D VI–VII 32–34. A 31–34   4 *tesselata*
                β Upper lateral line nearly reaching caudal fin.
D VI–VII, 33–36 A 32–34 16 to 19 gill-rakers on lower part of anterior arch. Eye 3½ to 4⅔ in length of head (in specimens of 125 to 250 mm.)
                                                                         5 *wiltoni*
D V (VI), 35–37 A 32–35 16 to 19 gill-rakers on lower part of anterior arch. Eye 4 to 4½ in length of head (in specimens of 90 to 180 mm.)
                                                                        6 *brevicauda*
D V–VI, 34–35 A 32–34 14 or 15 gill-rakers on lower part of anterior arch. Eye 3 to 3½ in length of head (in specimens of 130 to 180 mm.) 7 *longipes*
        3. Upper lateral line of 30 to 35 tubular scales, D V–VI, 28–31 A 27–30   8 *sima*
    B. Upper surface and sides of head scaly, including præorbital (and snout also except in *N. scotti*).
        1. Interorbital width 6 in length of head, D VI–VII, 32–33 A 35–36
                                                                          9 *lepidorhinus*
        2. Interorbital width 9 to 13 in length of head.
D IV–V, 36–37 A 32   10 *squamifrons*
D VI, 37–39 A 38   11. *larseni*
D V, 33 A 31   12 *scotti*

C. Upper surface and sides of head scaly (except in *N. nudifrons*), præorbital naked, interorbital width $\frac{1}{10}$ the length of head or less.

    1. Lower lateral line of 32 to 41 tubular scales, D VII-VIII, 31-33 A 31–33   13 *gibberifrons*

    2. Lower lateral line of 15 to 18 tubular scales, D VI-VII, 28–30 A 28–31   14 *acuta*

    3. Lower lateral line without tubular scales.

Upper surface of head scaly   D VII, 32   A 32   15 *vaillanti*
Upper surface of head scaly   D IV–V, 35–37   A 33–35   16 *mizops*
Upper surface of head naked   D IV–VI, 37–39   A 34–36   17 *nudifrons*

II. Opercles scaly above, naked below; upper surface of head scaly.

Interorbital width 10 in length of head   D VII, 29   A 27   18 *marionensis*
Interorbital width 20 in length of head   D V-VI, 29–30   A 30–31   19 *angustifrons*

III. Opercles scaled only on upper part of operculum; upper surface of head naked.

    A. Anal of 27–33 rays.

        a. Interorbital width 12 in length of head   D VI, 33   A 31   20 *elegans*

        b. Interorbital width 4 to 7 in length of head.

Cheek usually scaly behind eye   D IV–VI, 31–34. A 27–31   21 *cornucola*
Cheek scaly below and behind eye, its lower $\frac{1}{2}$ (young) or $\frac{1}{4}$ (adult) naked. D IV–VI 33–36   A 30–33   22 *cyaneobrancha*
Cheek scaly behind eye   D III–VII, 35–41   A 27–31   23 *coriiceps*

        c. Interorbital width $3\frac{1}{2}$ in length of head   D VI–VII, 33–35   A 27–29   24 *rossii*

    B. Anal of 22 to 25 rays, interorbital width $2\frac{1}{2}$ to $4\frac{1}{2}$ in length of head.

D IV, 29–31. 48 to 50 scales in a lateral longitudinal series   25 *macrocephala*

D VI–VII, 28–29. 52 to 58 scales in a lateral longitudinal series   26 *microlepidota*

D VI–VIII, 26–27. 84 to 92 scales in a lateral longitudinal series   27 *colbecki*

    C. Anal of 18 to 20 rays, interorbital width about 4 in length of head   28 *filholi*

(1) *Notothenia trigramma*, sp. n. (Pl. VI. fig. 2.)

Depth of body 5 in the length, length of head 4. Diameter of eye 5 in the length of head and equal to the interorbital width. Lower jaw projecting, maxillary extending to below anterior $\frac{1}{3}$ of eye; upper surface of head, except snout, cheeks and opercles scaly; 15 gill-rakers on lower part of anterior arch. Dorsal VI, 34. Anal 32. Pectoral longer than pelvics, $\frac{2}{3}$ as long as head, extending to above anal. Caudal rounded. About 85 scales in a lateral longitudinal series; 65 in upper lateral line, which nearly reaches caudal, 13 in line on middle of tail, and 40 to 45 in a third lower lateral line, which is separated by 4 or 5 longitudinal series of scales from the base of the anal fin. Brownish, fins darker.

Port Stanley, Falklands.

Total length 280 mm.

I was at first inclined to make this species the type of a new genus, but on examining related species of *Notothenia* I found a specimen of *N. brevicauda* with a third lateral line on one side only, formed of 10 tubular scales and separated from the posterior part of the anal fin by 3 series of scales.

(2) *Notothenia canina*

Smitt, *Bih. Sv. Vet.-Akad. Handl.* xxiii, iv, No 3, p 32, pl ii fig 23 (1897)

Evidently closely related to *N. tessellata*, but the outer series of teeth stronger, spaced, more canine-like, and the upper lateral line with 62 to 65 tubular scales. Dorsal VI 32–33. Anal 30–31.

East coast of Patagonia.

Total length 138 mm.

Notothenia acuta, Steind (*non* Gunther) (*Zool. Jahrb.*, Suppl iv, 1897–8, p 303), from Chile, is probably closely related to *N. canina*.

(3) *Notothenia ramsayi*, sp. n. (Pl VII fig 1.)

Depth of body 4 to $5\frac{1}{2}$ in the length of the fish, length of head about $3\frac{1}{2}$. Diameter of eye 4 to $4\frac{1}{2}$ in the length of head, interorbital width $4\frac{1}{2}$ to 7. Jaws equal anteriorly, maxillary extending to below anterior $\frac{1}{4}$ of eye; cheeks, opercles, and upper surface of head, to between the nostrils, scaly; 21 to 25 gill rakers on lower part of anterior arch. Dorsal VII (VIII), 34–36. Anal 32–34. Pectoral from less than $\frac{3}{5}$ to $\frac{2}{3}$ length of head; pelvics as long, extending to vent or to anal fin. Caudal rounded or subtruncate. Caudal peduncle as long as deep or deeper than long, its least depth $\frac{1}{4}$ to $\frac{2}{7}$ the length of head. 60 to 72 scales in a longitudinal series, from above base of pectoral to caudal fin; 46 to 54 in upper lateral line which almost reaches the caudal, 8 to 17 in lower lateral line. A lateral series of 5 to 7 dark blotches or vertical bars.

Several specimens, 200 to 300 mm in total length, taken on 1st December 1903 from the Burdwood Bank, *Scotia* Station 346, 54° 24′ S, 50° 32′ W, depth 56 fathoms, surface temperature 41.8° F; one from Isthmus Bay, Magellan Straits, 14 fathoms (COPPINGER).

This species is named in memory of ALLAN GEORGE RAMSAY, chief engineer of the *Scotia*, who died at Scotia Bay, South Orkneys, on 6th August 1903.

(4) *Notothenia tessellata*

Richards. "*Erebus*" and "*Terror*" *Fish.*, p. 19, pl. xii, figs. 3, 4 (1845); Günth., *Cat. Fish.*, ii, p. 260 (1860).
Notothenia veitchii, Günth., *Ann. Mag. Nat. Hist.* (4), xiv., 1874, p. 370.
„ *brevipes*, Lönnberg, *Swedish South Polar Exped.*, *Fish.*, p. 15 (1905).

Depth of body $4\frac{1}{4}$ to 6 in the length, length of head $3\frac{1}{4}$ to $3\frac{2}{3}$. Diameter of eye $4\frac{1}{2}$ to 6 in the length of head, interorbital width $5\frac{1}{2}$ to 6. Lower jaw rather prominent; maxillary extending to below anterior part or middle of eye; cheeks, opercles, and upper surface of head, except snout, scaly; 14 to 16 gill-rakers on lower part of anterior arch. Dorsal VI–VII, 32–34. Anal 31–34. Pectoral from less than $\frac{3}{5}$ to more than $\frac{2}{3}$ the length of head, usually longer than pelvics, which seldom reach the anal. Caudal rounded. Caudal peduncle deeper than long. 62 to 78 scales in a longitudinal series from above base of pectoral to caudal fin, 41 to 48 in upper lateral line, which ends below or a little behind end of dorsal fin, 6 to 11 in lower lateral line. Body marbled; spinous dorsal dusky, pale at the base; soft dorsal, caudal, and sometimes anal, with series of dark spots.

Chile; Magellan Straits; Falkland Islands.

Here described from several examples, 140 to 250 mm. in total length, from the Falkland Islands, Magellan Straits, and Chile, including the types of the species and specimens from Station 118, Port Stanley, Falkland Islands, collected by the *Scotia*. In young specimens (*N. veitchii*, *N. brevipes*) the interorbital width is $\frac{1}{4}$ or $\frac{1}{5}$ the length of head.

(5) *Notothenia wiltoni*, sp. n. (Pl. VII, fig. 2.)

Depth of body $4\frac{1}{4}$ to $5\frac{1}{2}$ in the length of the fish, length of head $3\frac{1}{3}$ to $3\frac{3}{5}$. Diameter of eye $3\frac{3}{4}$ to $4\frac{2}{3}$ in the length of head, interorbital width 6 to 7. Jaws equal anteriorly; maxillary extending to below anterior $\frac{1}{3}$ of eye or beyond; cheeks, opercles, and upper surface of head except snout, scaly; 16 to 19 gill-rakers on lower part of anterior arch. Dorsal VI–VII, 33–36. Anal 32–34. Pectoral $\frac{3}{4}$ or $\frac{4}{5}$ the length of head; pelvics as long or somewhat longer, extending to vent or to anal fin. Caudal rounded or subtruncate. Caudal peduncle deeper than long, its least depth $\frac{4}{7}$ to $\frac{1}{2}$ the length of head. 62 to 70 scales in a longitudinal series from above base of pectoral to caudal fin, 47 to 54 in upper lateral line, which almost reaches caudal, 7 to 14 in lower lateral line. Body with irregular dark cross-bars; spinous dorsal dusky, pale at base.

Ten specimens, 125 to 250 mm. in total length: one from Orange Bay (Paris Mus.), another from the Straits of Magellan (Coppinger), the others taken by the *Scotia* at Port Stanley (Station 118) and Port William (Station 349), Falkland Islands (shore, 51° 41′ S., 57° 51′ W.), and on the Burdwood Bank (Station 346, 54° 25′ S., 57° 32′ W., 56 fathoms, surface temperature 41·8° F., otter trawl, 1st December 1903).

This species is named after Mr. D. W. Wilton, zoologist of the *Scotia*.

(6) *Notothenia brevicauda*

Lonnberg, *Swedish South Polar Exped.*, *Fish*, p. 6, pl. v fig. 16 (1905).

Depth of body $4\frac{1}{2}$ to 5 in the length of the fish, length of head $3\frac{1}{3}$ to 4. Diameter of eye 4 to $4\frac{1}{2}$ in the length of head, interorbital width 7 or 8. Maxillary extending to below anterior $\frac{1}{3}$ of eye, cheeks, opercles, and upper surface of head, except snout, scaly, 16 to 19 gill-rakers on lower part of anterior arch. Dorsal V (VI), 35–37. Anal 32–35. Pectoral $\frac{5}{8}$ to $\frac{6}{8}$ the length of head, pelvics as long or a little longer, extending to the anal. Caudal rounded. Caudal peduncle $\frac{1}{2}$ to $\frac{3}{4}$ as long as deep, its least depth about $\frac{1}{3}$ the length of head. 60 to 70 scales in a longitudinal series from above base of pectoral to caudal fin, 44 to 50 in upper lateral line, which ends 2 to 4 scales in front of the caudal, 4 to 12 in lower lateral line. Body with irregular dark cross-bars; pectorals yellow, pelvics, anal, spinous dorsal, and base of soft dorsal dusky.

Magellan Straits, Falkland Islands.

Twelve specimens, 90 to 180 mm. in total length, including examples from Port Stanley (June 1903, 9–10 fathoms) and from Port William, Falkland Islands (January 1903, 6 fathoms). Lönnberg's type a specimen of 120 mm., came from Tierra del Fuego, and there are examples from that locality in the British Museum.

(7) *Notothenia longipes*

Steind., *Sitzungsb. Akad. Wien*, lxxiii, 1876, p. 70, pl. vi fig. 7 ; Günth., "*Challenger*" *Shore Fish*, p. 21 (1880).

Depth of body $5\frac{1}{2}$ to $6\frac{1}{2}$ in the length, length of head $3\frac{1}{3}$ to $3\frac{2}{3}$. Diameter of eye 3 to $3\frac{1}{2}$ in the length of head, interorbital width 7 or 8. Maxillary extending to below anterior $\frac{1}{4}$ of eye, upper surface and sides of head, except snout and preorbital, scaly. 14 or 15 gill-rakers on lower part of anterior arch. Dorsal V VI, 34–35. Anal 32–34. Pectoral $\frac{2}{3}$ to $\frac{5}{6}$ the length of head, somewhat shorter than pelvics, which reach the anal. Caudal rounded. Caudal peduncle $\frac{3}{5}$ to $\frac{4}{5}$ as long as deep, its least depth from $\frac{1}{4}$ to $\frac{1}{5}$ the length of head. 62 to 70 scales in a longitudinal series, 46 to 55 in upper lateral line, which almost reaches caudal, 6 to 13 in lower lateral line. Body with irregular brownish cross-bars.

Patagonia and Magellan Straits.

Here described from four examples 130 to 180 mm. in total length.

(8) *Notothenia sima*

Richards, *Erebus' and "Terror" Fish*, p. 19 pl. xi fig. 1 (1845). Günth., *Cat. Fish*, ii, p. 262 (1860).
Notothenia squamiceps, Peters, *Monatsb. Akad. Berlin*, 1876, p. 837.
,, *harlandreæ*, Lonnberg, *Swedish South Polar Exped.*, *Fish* p. 11, pl. iv fig. 13 (1905).

Depth of body 4 to 5 in the length, length of head $3\frac{1}{3}$ to $3\frac{2}{3}$. Diameter of eye 4 to 5 in the length of head, interorbital width 6 to 8. Maxillary extending to below anterior part or middle of eye, occiput, interorbital region, cheeks, and opercles scaly,

10 to 12 gill-rakers on lower part of anterior arch. Dorsal V-VI, 28-31. Anal 27-30. Pectoral ⅔ to ¾ the length of head, about as long as pelvics, which reach the vent. Caudal rounded. Caudal peduncle much deeper than long. 40 to 46 scales in a longitudinal series from above base of pectoral fin to caudal, 30 to 35 in upper lateral line, which ends below posterior rays of dorsal, 2 to 12 in lower lateral line when developed. Body with irregular dark cross-bars; vertical fins more or less dusky, the caudal often barred and with 2 or 3 dark spots at the base.

Magellan Straits, Falkland Islands.

Here described from several specimens, 60 to 120 mm. in total length, including the type of the species, from the Falkland Islands, and a co-type of *N. kerlandiea*.

The *Scotia* examples are from Station 118 Port Stanley, Falklands, 51° 41′ S. 57° 51′ W., and there are others in the British Museum collection from Magellan.

(9) *Notothenia lepidorhinus*

Notothenia lepidorhinus (part), Pappenheim, *Deutsche Sudpolar Exped*, XIII, Zool, v, p. 169, pl ix fig 1 and pl x fig 1 (1912)

Depth of body 4 to 4½ in the length, length of head 3½ to 3¾. Diameter of eye 3 to 3½ in the length of head, interorbital width about 6. Maxillary extending to below anterior margin of pupil; upper surface and sides of head, including snout and præorbital, scaly; 16 gill-rakers on lower part of anterior arch. Dorsal VI-VII, 32-33. Anal 35-36. Pectoral ⅞ the length of head; pelvics extending beyond origin of anal. Caudal rounded. Caudal peduncle somewhat deeper than long. 72 to 82 scales in a longitudinal series, 45 to 56 in upper lateral line, 32 to 38 in lower lateral line. Body with irregular dark cross-bars; spinous dorsal dark anteriorly, soft dorsal with dark oblique stripes.

Wilhelm Land, 385 metres.

The types measure 186 to 240 mm. in total length.

(10) *Notothenia squamifrons*

Gunth, "*Challenger*" *Shore Fish*, p 16, pl viii fig C (1880)

Depth of body 4½ in the length, length of head 3¾. Diameter of eye 3 to 3½ in the length of head, interorbital width 9 to 12. Maxillary extending to below anterior ¼ of eye; upper surface and sides of head, including snout and præorbital, scaly; 14 to 16 gill-rakers on lower part of anterior arch. Dorsal IV-V, 36-37. Anal 32. Pectoral ⅞ the length of head, rather shorter than pelvics, which reach the anal. Caudal peduncle deeper than long. 55 scales in a longitudinal series from above base of pectoral to caudal, 44 or 45 in upper lateral line, which ends below end of dorsal, or just behind it, 15 to 18 in lower lateral line. Body with broad irregular cross-bars; cheek with two oblique stripes; spinous dorsal blackish.

Kerguelen.

Here described from the types, two specimens, 110 and 150 mm. in total length.

(11) *Notothenia larseni*

Lonnberg, *Swedish South Polar Exped., Fish*, p 31, pl i fig 3 (1905)

Depth of body $4\frac{1}{2}$ to 5 in the length, length of head $3\frac{2}{3}$. Diameter of eye 3 in length of head, interorbital width 11 to 13. Maxillary extending a little beyond vertical from anterior margin of eye; upper surface and sides of head entirely scaly. Dorsal VI, 37–39. Anal 38. Pectoral a little shorter than head, longer than pelvics, which just reach anal. Caudal rounded. Caudal peduncle as long as deep. 69 to 76 scales in a longitudinal series above upper lateral line, which has 55 or 56 tubes and nearly reaches caudal; lower lateral line without tubes. Body with irregular cross-bars, dorsal with oblique series of spots.

South Georgia. length 178 mm

(12) *Notothenia scotti*

Boulenger, *Nat Antarct Exped Nat Hist*, ii *Fish*, p 2, pl i fig 1 (1907)

Depth of body $5\frac{1}{2}$ in the length, length of head $3\frac{1}{3}$. Diameter of eye $2\frac{1}{4}$ in the length of head, interorbital width 12. Maxillary extending to below anterior $\frac{1}{4}$ of eye; upper surface of head except snout, and sides of head, including præorbital scaly; 12 gill-rakers on lower part of anterior arch. Dorsal V, 33. Anal 31. Pectoral $\frac{3}{4}$ the length of head, somewhat shorter than pelvics, which reach anal. Caudal peduncle as long as deep. 50 scales in a longitudinal series from above base of pectoral to caudal, probably about 40 in upper lateral line. Body with irregular cross-bars, spinous dorsal blackish, soft dorsal and anal blackish posteriorly.

Near Edward Land

Here described from the type, a specimen of 110 mm, taken at a depth of 300 fathoms off the Ross Barrier 27th January 1902. In the original description and figure the fin-rays are miscounted.

(13) *Notothenia gibberifrons*

Lonnberg, *Swedish South Polar Exped., Fish*, p 23, pl iii fig 10 (1905), Vaillant, *Exped Antarct Française, Poiss*, p 33 (1906)

Depth of body 5 to $5\frac{1}{2}$ in the length, length of head $3\frac{1}{3}$ to $3\frac{1}{2}$. Diameter of eye 4 to $4\frac{2}{3}$ in the length of head, interorbital width 12 to 16. Jaws equal anteriorly, maxillary not or barely reaching vertical from anterior margin of eye; cheeks, opercles and upper surface of head to nostrils scaly; 10 gill-rakers on lower part of anterior arch. Dorsal VII–VIII, 31–33. Anal 31–33. Pectoral $\frac{3}{4}$ the length of head, pelvics $\frac{4}{5}$ to $\frac{4}{5}$ length of head, not reaching vent. Caudal truncate. Caudal peduncle nearly as long as deep. 55 to 66 scales in a longitudinal series from above base of pectoral to caudal, 36 to 44 (to 51 *fide* Lonnberg) in upper lateral line which ends below posterior part of dorsal, 32 to 41 in lower lateral line. Upper part of body irregularly spotted, dorsal, caudal and pectoral fins with series of dark spots. A water-colour drawing shows the ground colour yellow, the fins greenish, the spots brown.

Graham Land, South Georgia, South Orkneys, South Shetlands.

Here described from six specimens, 280 to 340 mm. in total length, taken in July 1903 at Station 325, Scotia Bay, 27 fathoms, and Station 326, Jessie Bay, 10 fathoms, South Orkneys; there are also two quite small specimens from the same locality. LÖNNBERG's types come from South Georgia, and there is a specimen in the British Museum from the South Shetlands.

(14) *Notothenia acuta*. (Pl. VIII. fig. 3.)

Günth., "*Challenger*" *Shore Fish.* p. 17 (1880). Pappenheim, *Deutsche Südpolar-Exped.*, xiii., *Zool.*, v. p. 171, pl. ix. fig. 3 (1912).

Depth of body 6 in the length, length of head 3½. Diameter of eye 3⅔ in the length of head, interorbital width 16. Maxillary extending to below anterior ¼ of eye; sides and upper surface of head scaly, except snout and preorbital. 12 gill-rakers on lower part of anterior arch. Dorsal VI (VII), (28–29) 30. Anal (28–30) 31. Pectoral nearly as long as the head, longer than pelvics, which reach the vent. Caudal peduncle somewhat deeper than long. 60 scales in a longitudinal series from above base of pectoral to caudal; 38 in upper lateral line, which ends below posterior part of dorsal; 16 to 18 in lower lateral line. Body marbled; dorsal rays with series of small spots; caudal barred.

Kerguelen.

Here described from the type, about 62 mm. in total length, from Kerguelen.

(15) *Notothenia vaillanti*, n. sp.

Notothenia acuta (non Günth.), Vaillant, *Exped. Antarct. Française, Poiss.*, p. 31 (1906).

Depth of body 5½ in the length, length of head 3¼. Diameter of eye 3 in the length of head, interorbital width 14. Maxillary extending to below anterior ¼ of eye; sides and upper surface of head scaly, except snout and preorbital. 10 gill-rakers on lower part of anterior arch. Dorsal VII, 32. Anal 32. Pectoral a little shorter than head, as long as pelvics, which reach the anal. Caudal peduncle a little longer than deep. 55 scales in a longitudinal series from above pectoral fin to caudal; 34 in upper lateral line, which ends below posterior part of dorsal; lower lateral line without tubular scales. Body with irregular cross-bars, broken up into 3 or 4 series of alternating spots; dorsal with small spots; caudal barred.

Graham Land, Booth, Wandel, and Wiencke Islands.

Here described from a specimen of 56 (46 + 10) mm. Measurements of this example are given by VAILLANT (*l. c.*, p. 32), and also those of a much larger fish, 410 mm. in length to base of caudal, with the eye ⅓ and the interorbital width $\frac{1}{10}$ of the length of the head.

(16) *Notothenia mizops*

Gunth., "*Challenger*" *Shore Fish*, p 16, pl viii fig D (1880)

Depth of body $4\frac{1}{3}$ to $4\frac{3}{4}$ in the length, length of head $3\frac{2}{3}$ to 4. Diameter of eye 3 to $3\frac{1}{2}$ in the length of head, interorbital width about 15. Maxillary extending to below anterior $\frac{1}{4}$ or $\frac{1}{3}$ of eye, cheeks, opercles, occiput, and interorbital region scaly, 9 to 13 gill-rakers on lower part of anterior arch. Dorsal IV V, 35–37. Anal 33–35. Pectoral $\frac{2}{3}$ to $\frac{3}{4}$ the length of head, pelvics longer, reaching the anal. Caudal rounded. Caudal peduncle deeper than long. 48 to 55 scales in a longitudinal series from above base of pectoral to caudal 33 to 38 in upper lateral line, which ends below posterior part of dorsal, lower lateral line without tubular scales. Body with 2 series of large, partly confluent, irregular blackish spots. cheek with 2 oblique stripes, a blackish spot on spinous dorsal, vertical fins with or without series of dark spots

Kerguelen

Here described from the types, five specimens, 70 to 170 mm in total length

(17) *Notothenia nudifrons*

Notothenia mizops var *nudifrons* Lonnberg *Swedish South Polar Exped, Fish*, p 30, pl i fig 2 (1905)
Notothenia mizops, Vaillant, *Expéd. Antarct Française, Poiss*, p. 30 (1906)

Closely related to *N mizops*, but occiput and interorbital region naked, fin-rays usually more numerous (Dorsal IV–VI, 37–39 Anal 34–36) and scales smaller, 55 to 65 in a longitudinal series, 11 or 12 gill-rakers on lower part of anterior arch. Coloration of *N mizops*. A water-colour drawing shows the fish reddish, the spots dark brown

South Georgia, South Orkneys, Graham Land

Here described from nine specimens, 70 to 150 mm in total length, from Station 325, Scotia Bay, South Orkneys, depth 9 to 10 fathoms (June 1903), from South Georgia (Swedish Expedition) and from Graham Land (Paris Mus)

18 *Notothenia marionensis* (Pl VIII, fig 2)

Gunth., "*Challenger*" *Shore Fish*, p 17 (1880)

Depth of body 5 in the length, length of head $3\frac{3}{4}$. Diameter of eye 4 in the length of head, interorbital width 10. Jaws equal anteriorly, maxillary extending to below anterior $\frac{1}{4}$ of eye, scales on upper half of cheek and opercles, on interorbital region and occiput, a transverse naked strip separating last from scales of nape, 11 gill-rakers on lower part of anterior arch. Dorsal VII 29. Anal 27. Pectoral fin $\frac{3}{4}$, pelvic $\frac{2}{3}$ the length of head. Caudal rounded or subtruncate. Caudal peduncle deeper than long. 48 scales in a longitudinal series from above base of pectoral to caudal fin, 35 in upper lateral line, which ends below posterior part of dorsal. 16 in lower lateral line. Body with irregular dark spots; a blackish spot on upper part of base of pectoral; dorsal and caudal with series of small spots.

Marion Island.

Here described from the type, 82 mm. in total length, from Marion Island 50 to 75 fathoms.

(19) *Notothenia angustifrons.* (Pl. VIII. fig. 1.)

Fischer, *Jahrb. Hamburg. Wiss. Anst.*, ii. 1885, p. 55.

Depth of body 5 in the length, length of head $3\frac{2}{3}$. Diameter of eye 4 in the length of head, interorbital width about 20. Maxillary extending to below anterior margin or anterior $\frac{1}{4}$ of eye; upper surface of head scaly to between nostrils, cheeks and opercles in great part scaly, but naked below; 10 or 11 gill-rakers on lower part of anterior arch. Dorsal V–VI 29–30. Anal 30–31. Pectoral nearly as long as head, longer than pelvics. Caudal rounded. Caudal peduncle about as long as deep. 46 to 52 scales in a longitudinal series from above base of pectoral to caudal, 26 to 33 in upper lateral line, which ends below middle or posterior part of soft dorsal, 16 to 23 in lower lateral line. Dark bars across the back, which break up into spots on the sides of the body, often a bar through spinous dorsal connecting the bases of the pectorals; dorsal, caudal and pectoral fins with series of small dark spots on the rays; pelvics and anal pale, sometimes with a few spots.

South Georgia, South Sandwich Islands.

Here described from six specimens, 70 to 116 mm. in total length, one from South Georgia (LÖNNBERG), the rest from the South Sandwich group (ALLARDYCE).

(20) *Notothenia elegans.*

Günth., "*Challenger* Shore Fish." p. 21, pl. xi. fig. C (1880).

Depth of body 6 to 7 in the length, length of head $4\frac{1}{3}$. Diameter of eye $3\frac{1}{2}$ in the length of head, interorbital width 12. Maxillary extending to below anterior $\frac{1}{3}$ of eye; a few scales behind eye and on upper part of operculum, rest of head probably scaleless; 10 gill-rakers on lower part of anterior arch. Dorsal VI, 33. Anal 31. Pectoral $\frac{3}{4}$ the length of head, rather shorter than the pelvics, which reach the anal. Caudal rounded. Caudal peduncle somewhat deeper than long. 46 to 48 scales in a longitudinal series from above base of pectoral to caudal, 40 or 41 in upper lateral line, which ends below last rays of dorsal, 4 to 9 in lower lateral line. Large dark spots or vertical bars on sides of body, tip of spinous dorsal pink, soft dorsal with 3 or 4 series of small dark spots.

Magellan Straits.

Here described from the types, two specimens 95 mm. in total length, from off Cape Virgins, Patagonia, 55 fathoms.

(21) *Notothenia cornucola*

Richards, "*Erebus*" and "*Terror*" *Fish*, pp 8, 18, pls viii figs 4, 5, and xi figs 3, 4 (1845), Gunth, *Cat Fish*, ii p 261 (1860)
Notothenia virgata, Richards, *l c*, p 18, pl xi figs 5, 6, Gunth, *l c*, p 262
    ,,   *marginata*, Richards, *l c*, p 18, pl xii figs 3, 4
    ,,   *modesta*, Steind, *Zool Jahrb Suppl*, iv, 1898, p 302, pl xx fig 3

Depth of body 3¾ to 4½ in the length, length of head 3 to 3½. Diameter of eye 4½ to 5 in the length of head, interorbital width 5¼ to 7. Jaws equal anteriorly, maxillary extending to below middle of eye, usually a few scales behind eye and on upper part of operculum. 11 or 12 gill-rakers on the lower part of anterior arch. Dorsal IV-VI, 31-34. Anal 27-31. Pectoral about ⅔ the length of head, extending to above origin of anal or a little beyond. pelvics about as long. Caudal rounded. Caudal peduncle much deeper than long. 47 to 55 scales in a longitudinal series from above base of pectoral to caudal, 36 to 42 in upper lateral line, which ends below last 2 or 3 rays of dorsal, 6 to 12 in lower lateral line, when it is developed, only 2 or 3 scales between lateral line and posterior rays of dorsal. Body usually spotted or marbled, sometimes with a pale lateral band. vertical fins dusky.

Patagonia, Magellan Straits, Falkland Islands. New Zealand, Chatham Islands.

Here described from numerous specimens, 90 to 140 mm in total length, including the types of the species, of *N virgata* and of *N marginata*, mostly from the Falkland Islands and Magellan Straits, one small specimen from New Zealand. Some examples were taken at Station 118, Port Stanley Falkland Islands shore, by the *Scotia*.

(22) *Notothenia cyanoebrancha*

Richards, "*Erebus*" and "*Terror*" *Fish*, p 7, pl iv (1844), Gunth, *Cat Fish*, ii p 261 (1860)
Notothenia purpuriceps, Richards, *l c*, pl ii figs 3, 4, Gunth, *l c* p 262

Depth of body 4 to 5 in the length, length of head 3 to 4. Diameter of eye 4 to 6 in the length of head, interorbital width 5 to 6. Jaws equal anteriorly, maxillary extending to below middle or posterior part of eye, upper surface of head naked except for a few temporal and post-temporal scales, which may be absent in the young, cheek scaly behind and below eye, the lower ½ (young) or ¼ (adult) naked, upper part of operculum scaly. 10 to 13 gill-rakers on lower part of anterior arch. Dorsal IV-VI, 33-36. Anal 30-33. Pectoral ⅔ the length of head, extending to above vent or origin of anal (adult) or a little beyond (young), pelvics about as long. Caudal rounded. Caudal peduncle much deeper than long. 60 to 70 scales in a longitudinal series from above base of pectoral to caudal, 32 to 39 in upper lateral line, which ends below posterior part of dorsal, lower lateral line, when developed, with 6 to 15 tubular scales. A dark oblique stripe from eye to angle of præoperculum, another below it.

Kerguelen

Here described from several specimens, 120 to 260 mm. in total length, including the type of the species.

(23) *Notothenia corniceps*

Richards, '*Erebus*' and '*Terror*' Fish, p. 5, pl. iii. figs. 1, 2 (1881); Gunth., *Cat. Fish*, ii. p. 261 (1860); Vaill., *Exped. Antarct. Française, Poiss.*, p. 24 (1906).

Depth of body $3\frac{2}{3}$ to $4\frac{1}{2}$ in the length, length of head 3 to $3\frac{1}{4}$. Diameter of eye $4\frac{1}{2}$ to 7 in the length of head, interorbital width 4 to 5. Jaws equal anteriorly, maxillary extending to below middle (young) or posterior margin (adult) of eye; head naked except for a few scales behind eye, on upper part of operculum, and on post-temporal region; 10 to 14 gill-rakers on lower part of anterior arch. Dorsal III VII, 35–40. Anal 27–31. Pectoral from less than $\frac{3}{4}$ (in large specimens) to $\frac{7}{8}$ the length of head, extending to above origin of anterior rays of anal; pelvics shorter, not or barely reaching vent. Caudal subtruncate. Caudal peduncle nearly as long as deep. 54 to 68 scales in a longitudinal series from above base of pectoral to caudal, 34 to 49 in upper lateral line, which ends below posterior part of dorsal, 8 to 17 in lower lateral line; 4 or 5 scales between lateral line and posterior dorsal rays. Colour varying from dark greenish black to a pale orange, with or without spots or marking; usually one or two oblique dark bars across cheek, sometimes broken up into spots; head sometimes with pale spots enclosed in dark rings; spots on body and dorsal fin sometimes large and tesselated, more often smaller and scattered, rarely uniting to form longitudinal stripes; soft dorsal and anal usually with a pale edge.

Graham Land and neighbouring islands; Kerguelen; Victoria Land.

Here described from a large series of specimens obtained by the *Scotia* at Station 325, Scotia Bay, South Orkneys, 160 to 450 mm. in total length; in addition to the type of the species from Kerguelen, examples from Duke of York Island and Cape Adare, Victoria Land (*Southern Cross*), and from Graham Land (*Français*).

(24) *Notothenia rossii*

Richards, '*Erebus*' and '*Terror*' Fish, p. 9 pl. v figs 1, 2 (1844); Gunth., *Cat. Fish*, ii. p. 263 (1860).

Macronotothen rossii Gill, *Proc. Acad. Philad.* 1861, p. 521.

Notothenia marmorata, Fischer, *Jahrb. Hamb. Wiss. Inst.*, ii, 1885, p. 53; Lönnberg, *Swedish South Polar Exped., Fish*, p. 34.

Depth of body $4\frac{1}{4}$ to $4\frac{1}{2}$ in the length, length of head $3\frac{2}{3}$ to $3\frac{3}{4}$. Diameter of eye 5 to $5\frac{1}{2}$ in the length of head, interorbital width $3\frac{1}{2}$. Jaws equal anteriorly, maxillary extending to below anterior margin of pupil; scales on upper part of cheek and operculum and on temporal region; upper surface of head papillose. 12 gill-rakers on lower part of anterior arch. Dorsal V VII, 33–35. Anal 27–29. Pectoral $\frac{3}{4}$ the length of head, longer than pelvics. Caudal truncate. Caudal peduncle as long as or a little longer than deep. 58 to 62 scales in a longitudinal series from above base of pectoral fin to caudal, 46 to 52 in upper lateral line, which ends below posterior rays of dorsal, 10 to 18 in lower lateral line. Body marbled, dorsal with 2 or 3 series of dark spots, anal and caudal with a dark band.

South Georgia, South Orkneys.

Here described from two specimens 250 mm in total length, from South Georgia, a little fish, 62 mm in total length, obtained by the *Scotia* at Station 325, Scotia Bay, South Orkneys seems to belong to this species.

Notothenia rossii was based on a large stuffed specimen, 850 mm in total length, with the dorsal spines short and blunt as they often are in large Notothenuds.

(25) *Notothenia macrocephala*

Gunth., *Cat Fish*, ii p 260 (1860)
Notothenia maoriensis, Haast, *Trans N Z Inst*, v, 1873, p 276, pl xvi fig
,, *angustata*, Hutton, *Ann Mag Nat Hist* (4) xvi 1875, p 313
,, *hassleriana*, Steind., *Sitzungsb Akad Wien* lxxii, 1876, p 69, pl vi fig
,, *antarctica*, Peters, *Monatsb Akad Berlin* 1876, p 837
,, *argyia*, Hutton, *Trans N Z Inst*, xi, 1879, p 339
,, *porteri*, Delfin, *Rev Chilen Hist Nat*, iii 1899, p 117

Depth of body 3 to 4 in the length, length of head $3\frac{1}{2}$ to $3\frac{3}{4}$. Diameter of eye 4 to 6 in the length of head, interorbital width $2\frac{1}{2}$ to $3\frac{1}{2}$. Jaws equal anteriorly, maxillary extending to below anterior $\frac{1}{4}$ of eye, imbricate scales behind eye and on upper part of operculum, upper surface and sides of head otherwise naked, papillose, 10 to 12 gill-rakers on lower part of anterior arch. Dorsal IV (III-VI), 29–31. Anal 22–25. Pectoral $\frac{3}{4}$ to $\frac{3}{5}$ the length of head, considerably longer than pelvics. Caudal truncate or slightly emarginate. Caudal peduncle usually somewhat longer than deep, 48 to 56 scales in a longitudinal series from above base of pectoral fin to caudal, 36 to 44 in upper lateral line, which ends below posterior rays of dorsal, 6 to 12 in lower lateral line. More or less distinct longitudinal stripes or series of spots on the sides, dorsal dusky, sometimes reticulated, caudal, anal, and pelvics sometimes similarly coloured.

Patagonia, Magellan Straits, Falkland Islands, New Zealand, Auckland Island, Campbell Island.

Here described from several specimens, 130 to 280 mm in total length, from New Zealand, Campbell Island, Magellan Straits, and the Falkland Islands. In addition to the type of the species, types of *N. argyia* and *N. angustata* have been examined.

(26) *Notothenia microlepidota*

Hutton, *Trans N Z Inst*, viii, 1876, p 213, Waite, *Subantarctic Isl N Zealand Pisces*, p 590, fig (1909)
Notothenia parva, Hutton *Trans N Z Inst*, xi, 1879 p 339

Depth of body 4 to 5 in the length, length of head $3\frac{1}{4}$ to $3\frac{1}{2}$. Diameter of eye $4\frac{1}{2}$ to $6\frac{1}{2}$ in the length of head, interorbital width $3\frac{1}{2}$ to $4\frac{1}{2}$. Upper surface of head naked, papillose; sides mostly naked, scaly behind the eye and on upper part of operculum. 11 or 12 gill-rakers on lower part of anterior arch. Dorsal VI–VII, 28–29. Anal 23–25. Pectoral ½ (adult) to ⅔ (young) the length of head; pelvics nearly as long, not reaching vent. Caudal rounded or subtruncate. Caudal peduncle deeper than long. 52 to 58 scales in a longitudinal series from above base of pectoral fin to caudal, 52 to 60 in upper lateral line, which ends near end of dorsal fin, 10 to 15 in lower lateral line. Head reticulated; body and fins spotted.

New Zealand; Auckland Island; Campbell Island.

Here described from five specimens, 90 to 500 mm. in total length, from Auckland and Campbell Islands; the smallest the type of *N. parva*.

(27) *Notothenia colbecki*.

Boulenger, 'Southern Cross' Pisces, p. 185, pl. xvi (1902); Waite, Subantarctic Isl. N. Zealand, Pisces, p. 594 (1909).

Depth of body 4 to 5 in the length, length of head 3½ to 3¾. Diameter of eye 5 to 7 in the length of head; interorbital width 3 to 4. Maxillary extending to below anterior part or middle of eye; head mostly naked, with granular papillæ, scaly behind the eye and on upper part of operculum. 15 to 18 gill-rakers on lower part of anterior arch. Dorsal VI–VIII, 26–27. Anal 23–24. Pectoral ⅔ to ⅞ the length of head, somewhat longer than pelvics, which do not reach the vent. Caudal emarginate. Caudal peduncle longer than deep. 84 to 92 scales in a longitudinal series from above base of pectoral to caudal, 62 to 69 in upper lateral line, which ends near end of dorsal fin, 24 to 35 in lower lateral line. Brownish above, yellowish below; a pair of oblique stripes across the cheek; dorsal and caudal dusky.

Auckland Island; Campbell Island.

Here described from specimens 125 to 550 mm. in total length, including the types from Campbell Island and a large stuffed specimen from Auckland.

(28) *Notothenia filholi*.

Sauvage, Bull. Soc. philom. (7), iv, 1880, p. 228; Passage de Venus, iii, p. 345 (1885); Vaillant, Exped. Antarct. Française, Poiss., p. 22 (1906).

Depth of body about 6 in the length, length of head 3½ to 4. Diameter of eye 4⅔ to 5 in length of head; interorbital width about 4. Head mostly naked, with granular papillæ, scaly behind the eye and on upper part of operculum. Dorsal VI–VII, 24–27. Anal 18–20. Caudal emarginate. Caudal peduncle longer than deep. Scales in a longitudinal series 100 to 110 (SAUVAGE) or 78 (VAILLANT), the discrepancy probably due to different methods of counting. Lower lateral line extending forward to above middle of anal, its anterior 15 scales overlapped by the upper. Brownish.

Campbell Island.

Total length 150 mm.

4 *Dissostichus*, Smitt, 1898

Bih Svensk Vet Akad Handl, xxiv, iv, No 5, p 1

Differs from *Notothenia* in that the teeth are uniserial spaced, canine-like
Patagonia to Graham Land

Dissostichus eleginoides

Smitt, *l c*, p 2 pl i figs 1–11, Vaillant, *Expéd Antarct Francaise, Poiss* p 36

Depth of body about 6 in the length, length of head 3. Diameter of eye about 5 in the length of head, interorbital width about $4\frac{1}{2}$ (? $5\frac{1}{2}$). Maxillary extending to below middle of eye, upper surface of head to nostrils, cheeks and opercles scaly. Dorsal IX–X, 27 28. Anal 28–30. Pectoral $\frac{3}{4}$ the length of head. Caudal truncate or slightly emarginate. Caudal peduncle much longer than deep. About 124 scales in a longitudinal series, upper lateral line extending back beyond dorsal, lower extending forward nearly to the pectoral

Total length of the type, 228 mm
Magellan Straits, Graham Land

5 *Eleginops* Gill, 1861

Proc Acad Philad, 1861, p 522

Eleginus (non Fischer), Cuv and Val, *Hist Nat Poiss*, v | 158 (1830) Gunth., *Cat Fish*, ii p 247 (1860)

This genus differs from *Notothenia* in the rather small mouth, in the complete absence of the lower lateral line, and in the shape of the pectoral fin

Chile, Patagonia, Falkland Islands

Eleginops maclovinus

Eleginus maclovinus, Cuv and Val, *l c*, Gunth, *l c*
" *chilensis*, Cuv and Val o c iv p 180 (1833), Gunth, *l c*
Aphritis undulatus, Jenyns, *Zool "Beagle," Fish*, p 160, pl xxix fig 1 Gunth, *t c*, p 243
" *porosus*, Jenyns, *l c*, p 162, Gunth, *l c*
Eleginus falklandicus, Richards, *'Erebus'* and *"Terror" Fish*, p 30, pl xx figs 1–3 (1815)

Depth of body $4\frac{1}{4}$ to $5\frac{1}{2}$ in the length, length of head $3\frac{1}{2}$ to 4. Diameter of eye 5 to 8 in the length of head, interorbital width 3 to 5. Maxillary just reaching vertical from anterior margin of eye in the young but not in the adult, occiput, interorbital region, cheeks and opercles scaly. 14 or 15 gill-rakers on lower part of anterior arch. Dorsal VIII IX, 24–26. Anal 22–24. Pectoral obliquely truncated, with the upper rays longest, nearly as long as head. Caudal truncate or emarginate. About 60 scales in a lateral longitudinal series, and 65 in the lateral line, which nearly reaches the caudal fin. Body often spotted or marbled

Chile, Patagonia, Falkland Islands
Here described from several specimens, 120 to 450 mm in total length

6. *Artedidraco*, Lönnberg, 1905.

Swedish South Polar Exped., Fish., p. 39.

Differs from *Notothenia* in the naked body, the absence of the lower lateral line, the presence of a mental barbel, the broad union of the gill membranes to the isthmus, and the hooked operculum.

Coasts of the Antarctic Continent and South Georgia.

(1) *Artedidraco mirus.*

Lönnberg, *t.c.*, p. 40, pl. i. fig. 4 and pl. iv. fig. 14.

Barbel club-shaped in the male. Depth of body 4 in the length, length of head $2\frac{3}{4}$ to $2\frac{7}{8}$. Diameter of eye $3\frac{1}{2}$ to 4 in the length of head, interorbital width $7\frac{1}{2}$ to $8\frac{1}{4}$. Dorsal III, 23–24. Anal 17.

Length of types 40 to 92 mm.

South Georgia.

(2) *Artedidraco skottsbergi.*

Lönnberg, *t.c.*, p. 48, pl. ii. fig. 7, pl. iv. fig. 15; Vaillant, *Exped. Antarct. Française, Poiss.*, p. 46 (1906).

Depth of body $4\frac{1}{2}$ to 5 in the length, length of head 3. Diameter of eye 3 to $3\frac{2}{3}$ in the length of head, interorbital width 9 or 10. Dorsal III, 24–25. Anal 18–19.

Graham Land. 125 m.

Length of type 57 mm.

(3) *Artedidraco shackletoni.*

Waite, *Brit. Antarct. Exped., Fish.*, p. 15, pl. ii. (1911).

Depth of body 4 in the length, length of head about 3. Diameter of eye $3\frac{3}{4}$ in the length of head, interorbital width 10. Dorsal V, 27. Anal 20.

Length of type 146 mm.

Victoria Land, off Cape Royds, Ross Island, 30 to 80 fathoms.

7. *Harpagifer*, Richards, 1844.

"Erebus" and "Terror" Fish, p. 11.

Differs from *Artedidraco* in the absence of the mental barbel and the development of the operculum and subopereulum as strong spines.

Patagonia to Graham Land and Kerguelen.

Harpagifer bispinis.

Batrachus bispinis (Callionymus bispinis, Forster), Schneid. *Bloch's Syst. Ichth.*, p. 45 (1801).
Harpagifer bispinis Richards, *t.c.*, pp. 11, 19, pls. vii. figs. 1–3, xii. figs. 8–9; Günth., *Cat. Fish.*, p. 263 (1860); Smitt, *Bihang Svensk. Vet.-Akad. Handl.*, xxiv., 1898, iv., No. 5, p. 17; Vaillant, *Exped. Antarct. Française Poiss.*, p. 44 (1906); Pappenheim, *Deutsche Südpolar Exped.*, xiii., Zool., v. p. 177 (1912).
Harpagifer palliolatus, Richards, *t.c.*, p. 20, pl. xii. figs. 5–7.

Dorsal III–V 21–25. Anal 16–20. Coloration variable, usually with bars or blotches.

Total length 100 mm

Patagonia, Magellan Straits, Graham Land, Falkland Islands, South Georgia, South Orkneys, Marion Islands, Kerguelen

The *Scotia* examples are from Station 118, Port Stanley, Falkland Islands, and Station 325, Scotia Bay, South Orkneys

Family 3 BATHYDRACONIDÆ

The depressed head, produced snout non-protractile mouth and absence of the spinous dorsal fin distinguish this family externally from the Nototheniidæ; the genera with spatulate snout may be distinguished from the Chænichthyids without a spinous dorsal fin by their scaly body

The skeleton of *Gymnodraco* differs from that of *Notothenia* in the more depressed skull and more produced rostrum, the elongation of the palatine which loses its lateral ethmoid attachment, and the separation of the mesopterygoid and the metapterygoid, so that the upper margin of the quadrate is free The pectoral arch is as in *Notothenia* There are 49 vertebræ (20+29), the præcaudals with parapophyses behind which the long slender epipleurals are inserted, and the feeble ribs attached to the epipleurals at some distance from the centra

I have ascertained that *Bathydraco* agrees with *Gymnodraco* in the structure of the palatine and of the pectoral arch and in the presence of ribs

Synopsis of the Genera

I Body scaly, snout spatulate, teeth villiform or cardiform, in bands, without canines

    A single lateral line running to or towards middle of base of caudal fin, body completely scaled   1 *Bathydraco*

    Lateral line running near base of dorsal fin, body completely scaled
         2 *Gerlachea*

    Lateral line running near base of dorsal fin, scales in scattered groups.
         3 *Racovitzaia*

II Body naked, snout pointed, teeth curved compressed, close set in a single series, with strong anterior canines   4 *Gymnodraco*

1 *Bathydraco*, Gunth, 1878
Ann Mag Nat Hist (5), II p 18

Body scaly, a single lateral line, running to or towards middle of base of caudal Snout spatulate, jaws with small villiform teeth in bands

Antarctic, in deep water

GUNTHER has stated 10 branchiostegals for *B antarcticus*, but I find only 7 DOLLO gives 6 for *B scotiæ*, but I count 7 in that species also

(1) *Bathydraco antarcticus*

Günth., *l.c.*, and 'Challenger' *Deep Sea Fish.*, p. 17, pl. vii. fig. A (1887).

Elongate, subcylindrical, the depth 9 in the length, length of head 3. Snout 1½ as long as diameter of eye, which is 4 in length of head, interorbital width 20. Lower jaw projecting, maxillary reaching vertical from anterior margin of eye, cheek completely scaled, 16 gill-rakers on lower part of anterior arch. Dorsal 36. Anal 31. Caudal subtruncate. Pectoral truncated, as long as head without snout, reaching origin of anal. About 140 scales in a lateral longitudinal series, about 60 in the lateral line, which is complete. Brownish, fins dusky.

South-east of Heard Island, 1260 fathoms.

Here described from the type, 260 mm. in total length.

(2) *Bathydraco macrolepis*

Boulenger, *Nat. Antarct. Exped. Nat. Hist.*, ii., *Fish.*, p. 4, pl. i. fig. 3 (1907).

Depth of body 9 in the length, length of head 3. Snout 1½ as long as diameter of eye which is 4½ in the length of head, interorbital width 14. Lower jaw projecting, maxillary reaching vertical from anterior margin of eye, cheeks naked below the suborbitals, 11 gill-rakers on lower part of anterior arch. Dorsal 34. Anal 29. Caudal subtruncate. Pectoral as long as head behind middle of eye, reaching origin of anal. About 90 scales in a lateral longitudinal series, about 55 in the lateral line which is complete. Brownish, fins dusky.

South-west of Balleny Islands, 252 fathoms.

Here described from the type, 210 mm. in total length. In the original description the number of gill-rakers was erroneously given as 6, and of dorsal rays as 39; the latter number is also shown in the figure.

(3) *Bathydraco scotiæ* (Pl. IX. fig. 4.)

Dollo, *Proc. Roy. Soc. Edin.*, xxvi., 1906, p. 65.

Depth of body 9 to 10 in the length, length of head 3⅙. Snout 1¾ as long as eye the diameter of which is 5 in the length of head, interorbital width 12 or 13. Lower jaw projecting, maxillary not reaching the vertical from anterior margin of eye, cheek naked below the suborbitals, 19 to 22 gill-rakers on lower part of anterior arch. Dorsal 38. Anal 31. Caudal subtruncate. Pectoral as long as head without snout, extending a little beyond origin of anal. About 100 scales in a lateral longitudinal series, 36 to 40 in the lateral line, which ends at a distance from the caudal equal to ½ its own length.

Two specimens, 133 and 145 mm. in total length, taken by the *Scotia* at Station 417 71° 22′ S., 16° 34′ W. off Coats Land depth 1410 fathoms, temperature 31°.9 F., trawl, 18th March 1904.

2. *Gerlachea*, Dollo, 1900

Bull Acad Roy Belg Sciences, p 195

Differs from *Bathydraco* in that the lateral line runs near the base of the dorsal fin, a second short lateral line above base of anal

Deep water off Graham Land

Gerlachea australis

Dollo, *l c*, p 196, and *Rés Voy "Belgica,"* Poiss, p 25, pl ii fig 1 and pl v fig 2 (1904)

Depth of body 5⅔ in the length, length of head 3¼ Snout twice as long as diameter of eye, which is 5 in the length of head, interorbital width 11 Maxillary not reaching vertical from anterior edge of eye, cheek fully scaled Dorsal 47 Anal 35 Pectoral ⅔ the length of head Caudal emarginate

71° 14′ S, 89° 14′ W, 246 fathoms

Total length 180 mm

3. *Racovitzaia*, Dollo, 1900

Bull Acad Roy Belg Sciences, p 317

Body with scattered groups of scales, a single lateral line running near base of dorsal fin, an incubatory pouch between pelvic fins and vent, in other characters similar to *Gerlachea*

Deep water off Graham Land

Racovitzaia glacialis

Dollo, *l c*, p 318 and *Rés Voy "Belgica"* Poiss, p 29, pl ii figs 2, 3, pl v fig 3 (1904)

Depth of body 12 in the length, length of head 3¼ Diameter of eye 4 in the length of head, interorbital width 25 Maxillary not reaching vertical from anterior margin of eye Dorsal 30 Anal 27

71° 19′ S, 87° 37′ W, 237 fathoms

Total length 82 mm

4. *Gymnodraco*, Boulenger, 1902

"Southern Cross" Pisces, p 186

Body naked, depressed anteriorly, compressed posteriorly Head depressed, snout produced, pointed jaws with curved compressed teeth close-set in a single series and with large anterior canines those of the mandible exposed in front of the snout Operculum with a strong spine with a hooked branch, suboperculum with a short spine, 6 branchiostegals, gill-membranes forming a fold across isthmus Two lateral lines

Coasts of the Antarctic Continent

Gymnodraco acuticeps

Bouleng., *l. c.*, p. xvii.—Pappenheim, *Deutsche Südpolar Exped.* xiii., Zool., v. p. 170, pl. ix. fig. 4 (1912).

Depth of body 8 in the length; length of head about 3. Snout as long as postorbital part of head. Diameter of eye 5 to 6 in length of head; interorbital width 6 to 7. Lower jaw strongly projecting; maxillary extending to below anterior margin of eye; gill-rakers short, sometimes almost vestigial except near the angle. Dorsal 28–30. Anal 24–26. Pectoral truncated, ½ as long as head. Caudal truncate. Large dark spots on head and body; fins dusky.

Victoria Land; Wilhelm Land.

Here described from the types, 200 to 300 mm. in total length, from Cape Adare, 1 to 3 fathoms.

Family 4. CHÆNICHTHYIDÆ.

This family differs externally from the Notothenidæ in the naked body, produced spatulate snout, and non-protractile mouth. The skeleton of *Champsocephalus esox* shows several peculiarities. The skull is depressed, with the long rostral lamina formed by the frontals and the ethmo-vomer; the parasphenoid meets the frontals between the small lateral ethmoids at the anterior margin of the orbit. The palatine is represented by the maxillary process, attached to the lateral edge of the rostral lamina near its anterior end, and by a posterior portion articulating with the lateral ethmoid, these being connected by a long and slender ligament; the pterygoid is slender, and there is no mesopterygoid. The præorbital is large, but the suborbitals are unossified. The pectoral arch is as in *Notothenia*. There are 57 vertebræ (28 + 29); the epipleurals are sessile, but the ribs are not ossified.

I have ascertained that *Chænichthys* and *Pagetopsis* are essentially similar in the structure of the rostrum, the palato-pterygoids and the pectoral arch, and in the absence of ribs. In all the genera the mouth is very distensible and the dentaries are freely movable on the articulars; this is the case, to a certain extent, in the Bathydraconidæ also.

Synopsis of the Genera.

1. Two lateral lines, pelvic fin-rays all branched or bifid, the middle ones the longest.
   A. Lateral line without bony plates, a spinous dorsal fin, subcontinuous with the soft dorsal.

   No spine on snout, spinous dorsal of 9 or 10 spines, not more than ⅓ the length of soft dorsal. .... 1. *Champsocephalus*

   A median spine near end of snout, spinous dorsal of 12 to 15 spines, more than ½ as long as soft dorsal. .... 2. *Pagetopsis*

   B. Lateral line with bony plates.

   A spinous dorsal fin .... 3. *Chænichthys*
   No spinous dorsal fin .... 4. *Parachænichthys*

II Two lateral lines, outer rays of pelvic fins longest, dorsal fins separated by
    an interspace lateral line without bony plates   5 *Chænocephalus*
III Three lateral lines
    Pelvic fins of moderate length   6 *Chionodraco*
    Pelvic fins elongate, the rays simple   7 *Cryodraco*

1 *Champsocephalus*, Gill 1861

Proc Acad Philad, p 509

Body naked, elongate, 2 lateral lines, without bony plates Eye nearly in middle of length of head no spine on snout Jaws with rather narrow bands of small sharp teeth, forming only 2 series laterally, lower jaw not projecting Gill-rakers short, but well developed on all the branchial arches dentigerous, about 20 on lower part of anterior arch Spinous dorsal fin well developed, its base less than $\frac{1}{3}$ that of the soft dorsal, with which it is almost continuous, pelvics comparatively short, with the rays normally branched, the middle ones the longest

Patagonia, Magellan Straits, South Georgia

(1) *Champsocephalus esox*   (Pl X fig 1)

Chænichthys esox, Gunth, *Ann Mag Nat Hist* (3), vii, 1861 p 89

Depth of body 7 to 8 in the length, length of head 3 to $3\frac{1}{2}$ Snout a little longer than postorbital part of head Diameter of eye 7 in the length of head, interorbital width 4 to 5 Supraorbital edges not raised Maxillary extending to below anterior part or middle of eye Uppermost opercular spine shorter than and quite distinct from the middle one Dorsal (IX) X, 33–36 Anal 32–35

Body with dark cross-bars

Patagonia, Magellan Straits

Here described from five specimens, 200 to 300 mm in total length, including the type of the species

(2) *Champsocephalus gunnari*   (Pl X fig 2)

Lonnberg, *Swedish South Polar Exped*, *Fish*, p 37 (1905)

Depth of body $6\frac{1}{2}$ in the length, length of head $3\frac{1}{2}$ Snout as long as postorbital part of head Diameter of eye 5 in the length of head, interorbital width $3\frac{1}{2}$ Supraorbital edges not raised Maxillary extending to below anterior $\frac{1}{3}$ of eye Uppermost and middle opercular spines only free distally, appearing as a single bifid spine Dorsal IX (X), 37–40 Anal 36–38 Plumbeous, with some broad darker cross-bars

South Georgia

Here described from a specimen of 420 mm

2. Pagetopsis, gen. nov.

Body naked, moderately elongate; two lateral lines, without bony plates. Eye behind middle of length of head; an antrorse curved spine near end of snout. Teeth in jaws small, sharp, biserial; lower jaw slightly projecting; gill-rakers vestigial or absent. Spinous dorsal fin well developed, its base more than ½ that of the soft dorsal; pelvics rather long, the rays bifid or slightly branched.

Coasts of the Antarctic Continent.

Pagetopsis macropterus.

Champsocephalus macropterus Boulenger, *Nat. Antarctic Exped. Nat. Hist.*, II, *Fish.* p. 3, pl. i.; Pappenheim, *Deutsche Südpolar-Exped.* XIII, *Zool.* v. p. 174 (1912).

Depth of body 4 to 5 in the length, length of head 2½ to 2¾. Snout nearly ½ the length of head. Diameter of eye 5 in the length of head; interorbital width 4. Maxillary extending to below anterior ⅓ of eye. 3 or 4 opercular spines, the uppermost with an antrorse hook. Dorsal XII–XV 28–31. Anal 25–27. Pectoral ⅔, pelvics ⅔ the length of head. Dark spots and vermiculations on head; irregular double cross-bars on body.

Victoria Land; Wilhelm Land.

Here described from the types 160 to 250 mm. in total length, from the stomach of a seal near Cape Armitage, Ross Island.

3. Chænichthys, Richards., 1844.

"*Erebus*" *and* "*Terror*" *Fish*, p. 12; Günth. *Cat. Fish.*, II p. 249 (1860).

Differs from *Champsocephalus* in having a spine on the snout, the teeth in broader bands and in the bony plates of the lateral line. Dorsal fins separated by an interspace. Gill-rakers short, dentigerous.

Kerguelen.

(1) Chænichthys rhinoceratus.

Richards., *l.c.*, p. 13, pl. vi.; Günth., *Cat. Fish.*, II p. 249 (1860); Pappenheim, *Deutsche Südpolar-Exped.*, XIII, *Zool.*, v. p. 193.

Depth of body 6 in the length, length of head 2¾. Snout nearly ½ the length of head. Diameter of eye 5½ to 6½ in the length of head; interorbital width 5 to 5½. Maxillary extending beyond middle of eye (adult). Head moderately rugose; supraorbital edges slightly raised. Dorsal VII, 33–34. Anal 30–33. Second and third rays of spinous dorsal longest, thence decreasing rapidly. 79 to 84 plates in upper lateral line; a few plates on middle of side. Brownish, with darker spots and reticulations.

Description from the type, a specimen of 450 mm. and a second example of 175 mm., from Kerguelen.

(2) *Chænichthys rugosus*, sp. n.

Eye smaller than in *C. rhinoceratus*, diameter 8 in head. Head rougher and supraorbital edges more elevated. Maxillary shorter, not quite reaching middle of eye. Dorsal VIII, 30; third and fourth spines longest, fifth as long as first. Anal 29. 62 plates in upper lateral line, a nearly continuous series of plates on middle of side.

A specimen of 400 mm. from Kerguelen.

A stuffed example with VIII, 34 dorsal and 30 anal rays, and 72 plates in the lateral line, appears to belong to this species.

4. *Parachænichthys*, Bouleng., 1902

"*Southern Cross*" *Pisces*, p. 176

Differs from *Chænichthys* in the absence of the spinous dorsal fin.
South Georgia, Graham Land.

Parachænichthys georgianus

Chænichthys georgianus, Fischer, *Jahrb. Hamburg Wiss. Anstalt*, i., 1885, p. 50, pl. i. figs. 1, 2
? ,, ,, *Marcotti*, Vaillant, *Exped. Antarct. Française Poiss.*, p. 39, fig.

Maxillary not nearly reaching the vertical from anterior margin of eye. Interorbital region narrow, its width less than $\frac{1}{2}$ the diameter of eye. Dorsal 44. Anal 32.

South Georgia. Graham Land.

Total length 490 mm.

It seems probable that the imperfect fish described by Vaillant, from Graham Land, belongs to this species. The figure of the upper surface of the head is at first sight rather different from Fischer's but the differences may be due to the expansion of the jaws and opercles and the smaller size of the specimen (head 136 as against 173 mm.)

5. *Chænocephalus*, gen. nov.

Body naked, elongate, two lateral lines without distinct bony plates. Eye somewhat behind middle of head; a small prominence at anterior end of ethmoid; jaws with small sharp teeth forming rather broad bands, there being several series even at the sides; lower jaw not projecting; gill-rakers absent except for 3 or 4 very short ones below the angle of the first arch. Spinous dorsal fin well developed, its base about $\frac{1}{4}$ that of the soft dorsal, from which it is separated by an interspace; pelvics comparatively short, with the two outer rays the longest, enveloped in thick skin, but bifid, the others normally branched.

South Georgia.

Chænocephalus aceratus (Pl. XI.)

Chænichthys aceratus Lönnberg, *Kungl. Svensk. Vet.-Akad. Handl.*, xl, 1906, No. 5, p. 97.

Depth of body 5 to 6 in the length, length of head 2⅓ to 2¾. Snout a little less than ⅓ the length of head. Diameter of eye 5 to 6 in the length of head; interorbital width about 5. Supraorbital edges raised; operculum with 3 radiating ridges ending in spines, the uppermost bifid. Maxillary extending to below middle of eye or beyond. Dorsal VII-VIII, 39-40; third spine longest, ⅔ to more than ¾ the length of head. Anal 37-38. Pectoral and pelvic fins subequal in length, nearly ½ the length of head. Greyish, with 4 or 5 dark cross bands, the first from spinous dorsal through base of pectoral, the second downwards from origin of soft dorsal; the others less regular and sometimes with narrower bars developed between them.

South Georgia.

Four specimens, 480 to 530 mm. in total length, collected by Mr. DAVID FERGUSON, and presented to the Scottish Oceanographical Laboratory by Messrs. SALVESEN.

6. *Chionodraco*, Lönnberg, 1906.

Kungl. Svensk. Vet. Akad. Handl., xl, No. 5, p. 99.

Apparently intermediate between *Chænocephalus* and *Cryodraco*, resembling the former in fin-structure, the latter in the three lateral lines and the well-developed rostral spine.

Graham Land.

Chionodraco hamatus

Chænichthys rhinoceratus subsp. *hamatus*, Lönnberg, *Swedish South Polar Exped., Fish.* p. 47 (1905).
Chionodraco hamatus, Lönnberg, *Kungl. Svensk. Vet. Akad. Handl.* xl, 1906, No. 5, p. 99.

Head 3 in total length (with caudal). Snout nearly ½ length of head, nearly twice diameter of eye, and 1¾ interorbital width. Dorsal VII, 37. Anal 33.

Snow Hill.

Total length 330 mm.

7. *Cryodraco*, Dollo 1900.*

Bull. Acad. Roy. Belg. Sciences, p. 129.

Differs from *Chænocephalus* especially in the structure of the pelvic fins, with the rays simple, the two outer enlarged and prolonged, and in the presence of an additional lateral line at the base of the anal fin.

Graham Land, Wilhelm Land.

(1) *Cryodraco antarcticus*

Dollo, *l. c.*, p. 130, and *Rés. Voy. "Belgica," Poiss.*, p. 20, pl. i, pl. v, fig. 7 (1904).

Depth of body 8 in the length, length of head 3⅓. Snout 2, eye 4, interorbital width 5 in the length of head. Dorsal III, 44. Anal 43. Pelvic fin more than ½ the length

---

* A fish from Wilhelm Land, 69 mm. long, is recorded by PAPPENHEIM under the name *Pagetodes antarcticus*. The number of fin-rays (D IV, 31 A 31) scarcely justifies this determination and the fish may well belong to an undescribed species. But as it is so juvenile and even its generic position uncertain, I refrain from giving it a specific name.

of the fish, extending nearly to end of dorsal fin. Body with 7 dark transverse bands.

71° 18' S., 88° 2' W., 450 metres.
Total length 200 mm.

(2) *Cryodraco pappenheimi*, sp. n.

*Pagetodes * antarcticus* (non Dollo), Pappenheim, *Deutsche Südpolar Exped.*, xiii., *Zool.*, v. p. 175.

Length of head 2¾ in the length of the fish. Snout 2 in the length of head, diameter of eye 5, interorbital width 4. Dorsal V, 45. Anal 39. Pelvics only reaching fourteenth ray of dorsal (the prolonged rays perhaps not entire).

Wilhelm Land.

Length of the type, 168 mm. to base of caudal. This species is known to me only from Dr. PAPPENHEIM's description and from some notes and measurements that he has kindly sent me. Some of these may be given for comparison with those of the type of *C. antarcticus*. The measurements are in millimetres.

	Length to Base of Caudal	Head to End of Opercular Flap	Head to End of Bony Operculum	Snout	Eye	Interorbital Width
C. antarcticus	173	156	53	26.5	13.25	10.6 †
C. pappenheimi	168	68	?64	32	13	16

IV. THE SYSTEMATIC POSITION AND GEOGRAPHICAL DISTRIBUTION OF THE GALAXIIDÆ AND HAPLOCHITONIDÆ.

The Galaxiidæ and Haplochitonidæ are Teleostean fishes of the order Isospondyli, that is to say, they are malacopterous physostomes with a truly homocercal caudal fin, with abdominal pelvic fins, and with ribs inserted on autogenous parapophyses. In this order the name Salmonoid may be given to a group of fishes with an adipose fin usually present, with one supramaxillary or none, with parietals well developed, and with oviducts absent or incomplete. The relations of the Salmonoid families are indicated in the following synopsis:—

  I. An orbitosphenoid, an opisthotic, a mesocoracoid, vertebræ upturned at base of caudal fin.   1. *Salmonidæ*.
  II. An orbitosphenoid, no opisthotic, no upturned vertebræ, meso-pterygoids toothless.
    A. mesocoracoid, parapophyses inferior   2. *Argentinidæ*.
    No mesocoracoid, parapophyses lateral   3. *Microstomidæ*.

---

* The fish named *Pagetodes* by RICHARDSON ("*Erebus*" and "*Terror*" *Fish.*, p. 15, pl. viii. fig. 3) may have belonged to the genus *Cryodraco*, but in the form of the body, the length of the pelvic fins, and the continuous dorsals it shows more resemblance to *Pagetopsis*. Until RICHARDSON's species is rediscovered, the name *Pagetodes* cannot be used.

† DOLLO's figure of the upper surface of the head is enlarged, the length of the head, to the end of the bony operculum, to 80 mm. and the interorbital width to 16 mm.

III. No orbitosphenoid no opisthotic; no upturned vertebræ, mesopterygoids toothed (absent in Salangidæ)
A. A mesocoracoid, maxillaries dentigerous, entering gape ... 4. *Osmeridæ*.
B. No mesocoracoid, maxillaries dentigerous entering gape
 Head compressed, mesopterygoid well developed, dentigerous ribs ossified ... 5. *Retropinnatidæ*
 Head strongly depressed, no mesopterygoid, ribs not ossified 6. *Salangidæ*
C. No mesocoracoid, maxillaries toothless, behind præmaxillaries
 Præmaxillaries not extending whole length of maxillaries, roof of myodome unossified, no adipose fin ... 7. *Galaxiidæ*
 Præmaxillaries nearly reaching extremities of maxillaries, roof of myodome ossified, an adipose fin ... 8. *Haplochitonidæ*

The Argentinidæ and Microstomidæ are inhabitants of rather deep water, but the rest are littoral fishes, many of them entering fresh water and often forming colonies, races, or species confined to fresh water.

It is of some interest to note that the Galaxiidæ and Haplochitonidæ are related to, but more specialised than, the Osmeridæ, or Smelt family, of northern seas. *Retropinna*, from the coasts and rivers of Australia and New Zealand, is still nearer to the Galaxiidæ and Haplochitonidæ, both these families occur in Australia, Tasmania, New Zealand, South America, and the Falkland Islands and there are even two species of *Galaxias* at the Cape of Good Hope. All the species enter fresh water and the majority seem to be strictly fluviatile or lacustrine, but in a few cases species of *Galaxias* have been observed in the sea.

In 1906 (*Proc. Zool. Soc.*, 1905, ii. pp. 363-384, pls. x-xiii.) I published a revision of the Galaxiidæ, and then wrote :—

' The occurrence of *Galaxias maculatus* in the sea has been recorded by VALENCIENNES and by PHILIPPI, off the Falkland Islands and off the coast of Chile respectively. The observations of JOHNSTON in Tasmania and of HUTTON and CLARKE in New Zealand are to the effect that *Galaxias attenuatus* descends to the sea periodically to spawn. Mr. RUPERT VALLENTIN has seen shoals of little fishes, which I identify with the *Galaxias gracillimus* of CANESTRINI in the sea at the Falkland Islands. Recently *Galaxias brevipinnis* also has been found to be marine, *G. hollansi* described by HUTTON from the Auckland Islands, proving to be identical with this species'

WAITE (*Subantarctic Islands of New Zealand*, p. 586) has recently shown that HUTTON's conclusion as to the marine habit of *G. brevipinnis* was probably incorrect. EIGENMANN (*Rep. Princeton Exped. Patagonia*, iii., Zool., 1909, p. 274) says of *G. gracillimus* "This is undoubtedly the young of *attenuatus*", and if this opinion, which does not appear to be the result of an examination of specimens, be accepted, the known marine species of *Galaxias* would be reduced to two only.

In my revision I distinguished *G. gracillimus* from *G. attenuatus* by the more slender form, the smaller head etc. My specimens, 53–55 mm in total length, were of the same size as the smallest examples of *G. attenuatus*, but, bearing in mind the extraordinary larval history of *Anguilla*, *Albula*, etc., I wrote ' Possibly this species may be based on a larval form of *G. attenuatus*, but if so it is remarkable that it has been recorded only from South America, and that larval forms of other species have not been described.' A series of *Galaxias attenuatus* from the Falkland Islands, since received from Mr VALLENTIN, includes specimens of 20 to 30 mm which agree with those of 55 to 60 mm in form, size of head, etc., and show pretty conclusively that *G. gracillimus* does not represent a stage in the life-history of this species. Mr VALLENTIN'S collection also includes some young examples of *G. smithii*, hitherto known only from the type from Sir ANDREW SMITH'S collection; these are yellowish, with numerous brownish irregular vertical stripes.

The South American species of *Galaxias* are seven in number, viz.—

1. *Galaxias attenuatus*, Jenyns, 1842

S.E. Australia, Tasmania, New Zealand and neighbouring islands, Chile, Patagonia, Tierra del Fuego, Falkland Islands.

2. *Galaxias gracillimus*, Canestrini, 1864

Chile, Falkland Islands.

3. *Galaxias maculatus*, Jenyns, 1842

Chile, Patagonia, Tierra del Fuego, Falkland Islands.

4. *Galaxias alpinus*, Jenyns, 1842

Alpine lakes of Tierra del Fuego.

5. *Galaxias bullocki*, Regan, 1908

Ann. Mag. Nat. Hist. (8), i. p. 372.

Temuco, Chile.

6. *Galaxias platei*, Steind., 1897

Galaxias titcombi, Everm. and Kendall, Proc. U.S. Nat. Mus., xxxi, 1907, p. 92, fig.

Patagonia, Argentina.

7. *Galaxias smithii*, Regan, 1906

Falkland Islands.

It should be noted that only the marine species occur both at the Falkland Islands and on the continent of South America, and there can be little doubt that *Haplochiton zebra*, with this distribution, will prove to be marine.

The conclusion that the Galaxiidæ are originally marine and are establishing themselves in fresh water is strengthened by their relationship to the Osmeridæ; their distribution has little bearing on the question of a former extension of the Antarctic Continent.

The expense of the publication of this Memoir is defrayed from the Government Publication Grant administered by the Royal Society of London.

LIST OF THE PLATES

Plate I
Raia magellanica × ½

Plate II
Fig 1 *Chalinura ferrieri*
Fig 2 ,, *whitsoni*

Plate III
Fig 1 *Cynomacrurus piriei*
Fig 2 *Neobythites brucei*

Plate IV
Fig 1 *Bovichthys angustifrons*
Fig 2 *Cottoperca macrophthalma*
Fig 3 ,, *gobio*

Plate V
Fig 1 *Austronycus depressiceps*
Fig 2 *Cottoperca macrophthalma* × ¼

Plate VI
Fig 1 *Ursoperca coatsii*
Fig 2 *Notothenia trigramma* × ½

Plate VII
Fig 1 *Notothenia ramseyi*
Fig 2 ,, *wiltoni*

Plate VIII
Fig 1 *Notothenia angustifrons*
Fig 2 ,, *martonensis*
Fig 3 ,, *acuta* × 1¼
Fig 4 *Trematomus loennbergi*
Fig 5 *Synaphobranchus australis*

Plate IX
Fig 1 *Bovichthys decipiens* × 1¼
Fig 2 *Bathylagus glacialis*
Fig 3 *Lycenchelys antarcticus*
Fig 4 *Bathydraco scotiae*
Fig 5 *Bovichthys dracanthus*

Plate X
Fig 1 *Champsocephalus esox*
Fig 2 ,, *gunnari* × 7/12

Plate XI
Chanocephalus aceratus

Trans. Roy. Soc. Edin^r REGAN: "SCOTIA" ANTARCTIC FISHES. PL. II. Vol. XI

1. CHALINURA FERRIERI. 2. CHALINURA WHITSONI.

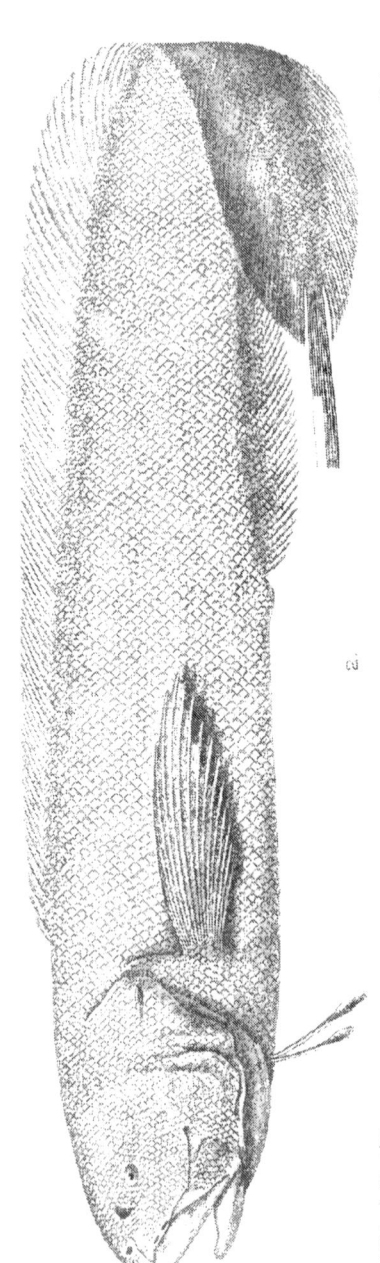

1. CYNOMACRURUS PIRIEI.   2. NEOBYTHITES BRUCII

Trans. Roy. Soc. Edin^r. REGAN. "SCOTIA" ANTARCTIC FISHES. PL. IV.

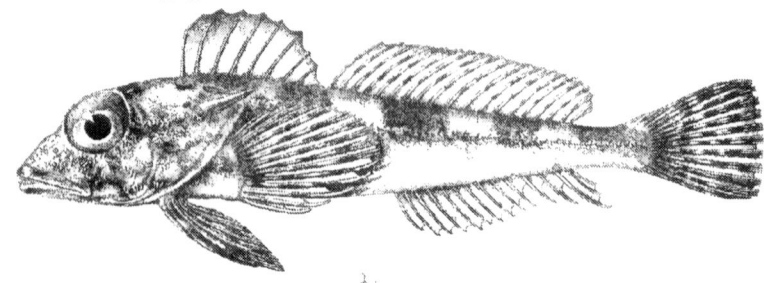

1.

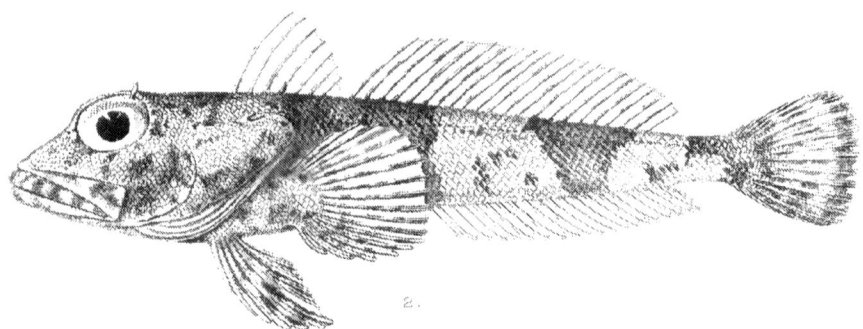

2.

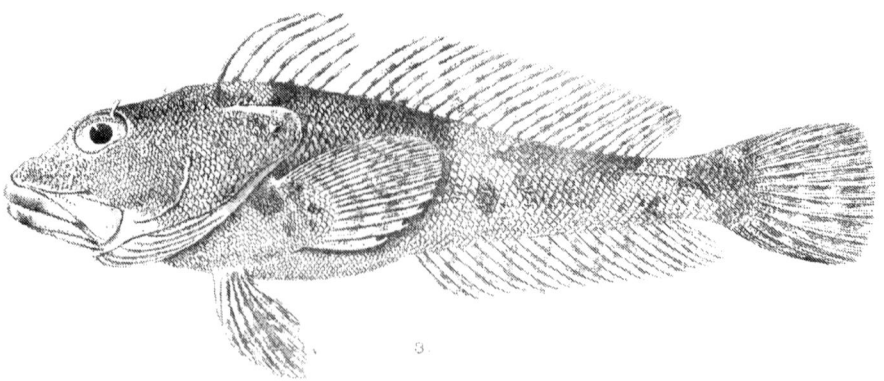

3.

1. BOVICHTHYS ANGUSTIFRONS.
2. COTTOPERCA MACROPHTHALMA. 3. C. GOBIO.

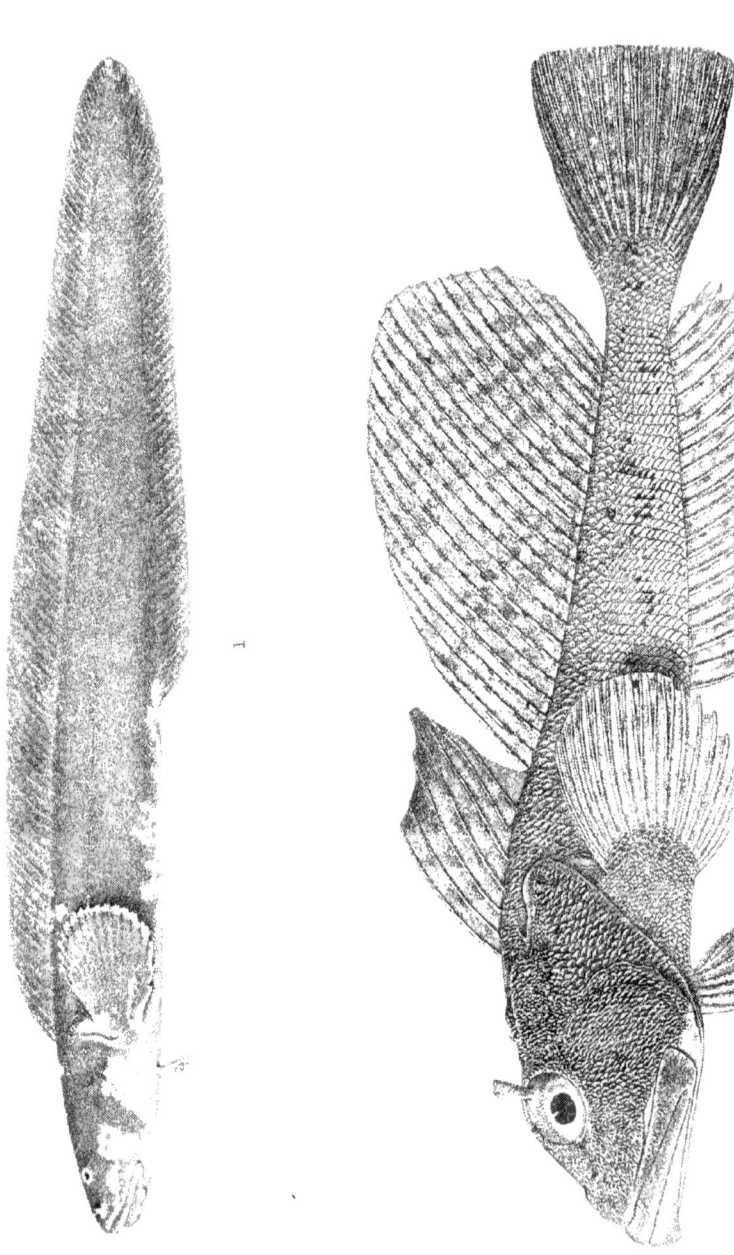

1. AUSTROLYCUS DEPRESSICEPS. 2. COTTOPERCA MACROPHTHALMA. ADULT.

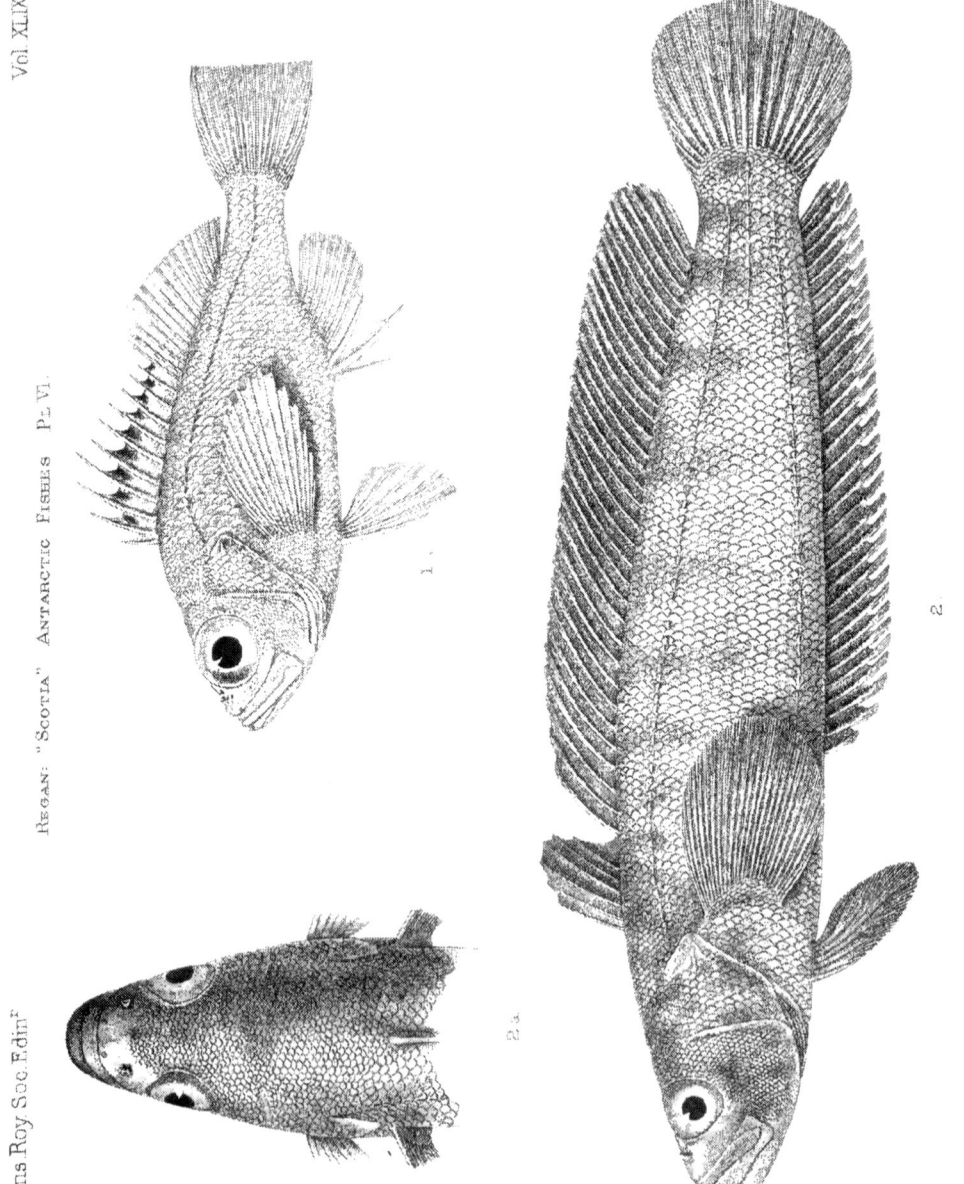

1. CAESIOPERCA COATSII. 2. NOTOTHENIA TRIGRAMMA.

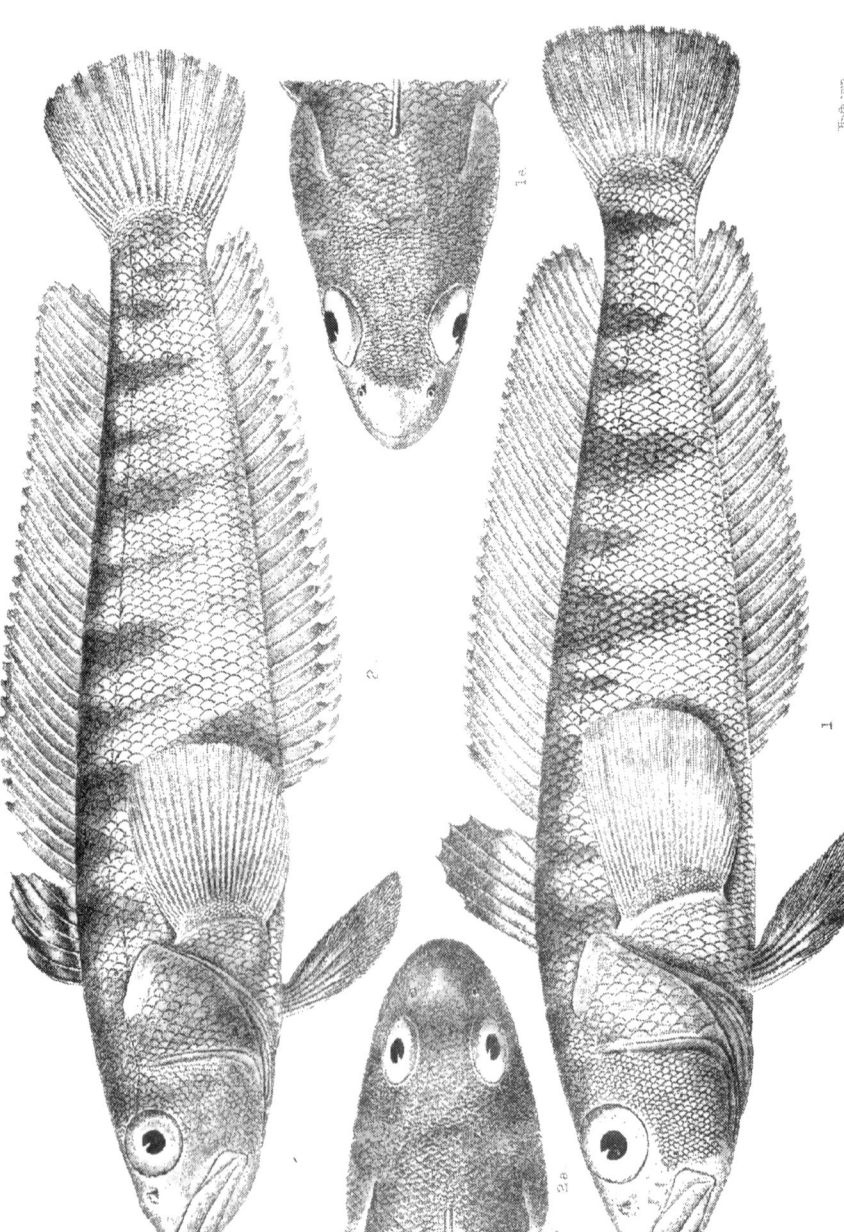

1. NOTOTHENIA RAMSAYI.   2. NOTOTHENIA WILTONI.

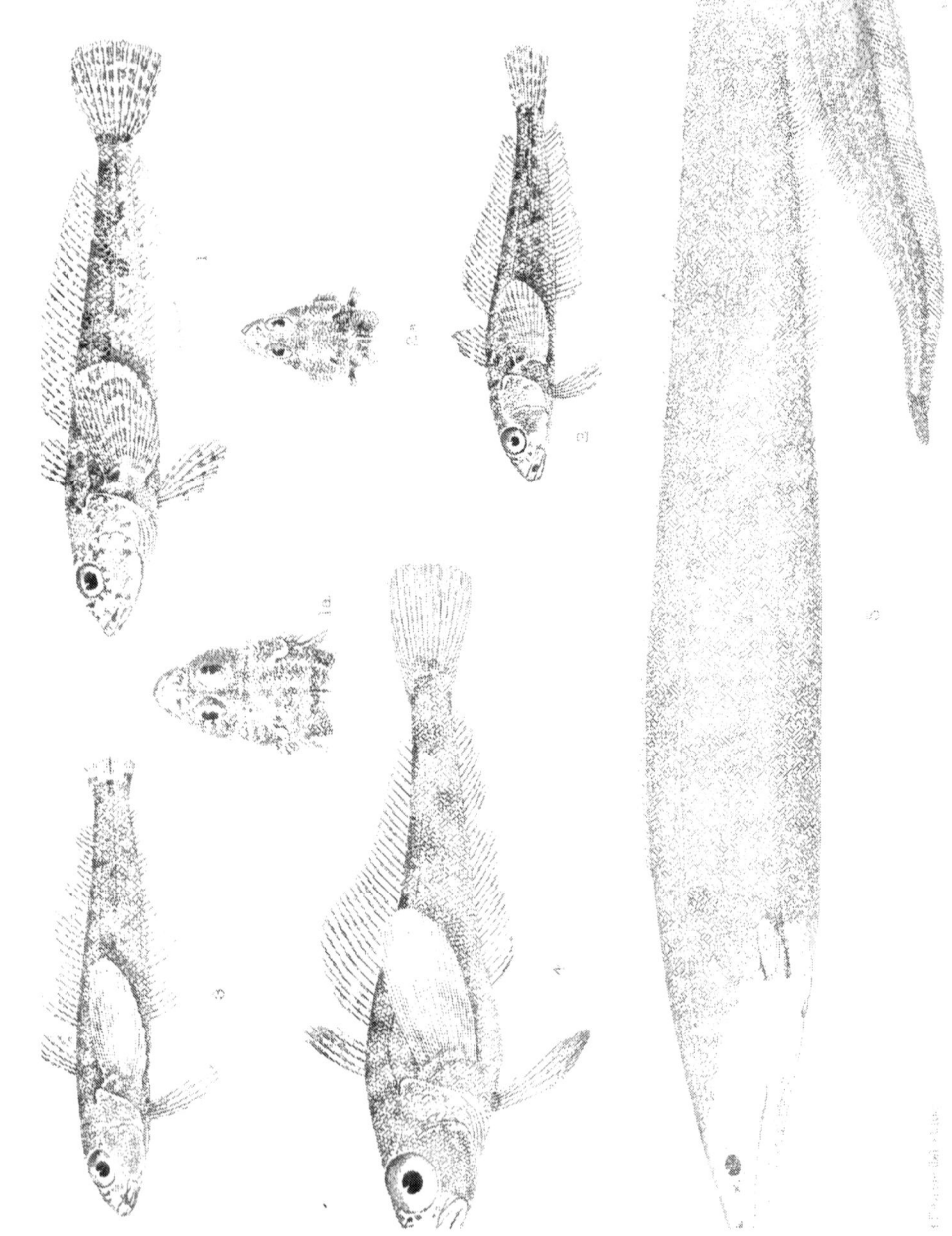

1. BOVICHTHYS DECIPIENS 2. BATHYLAGUS GLACIALIS.

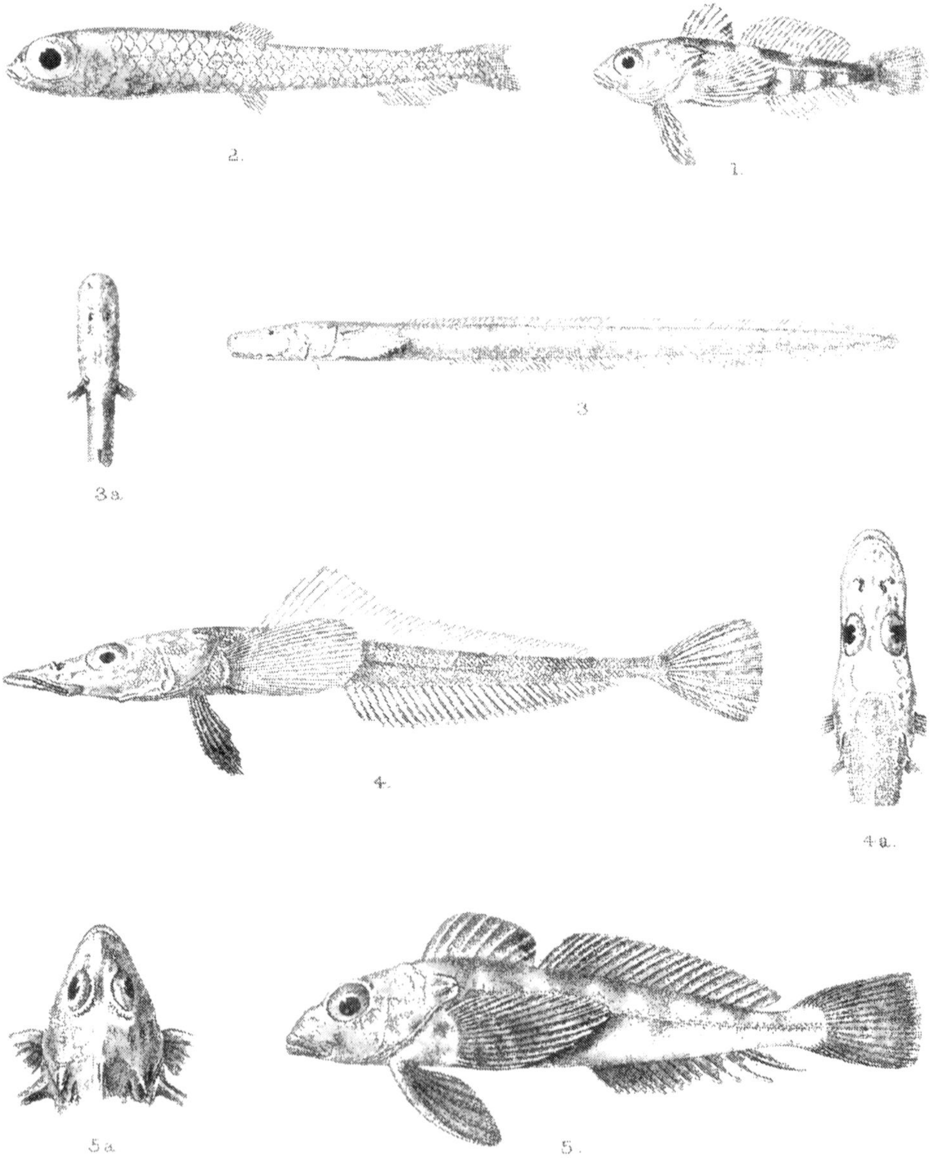

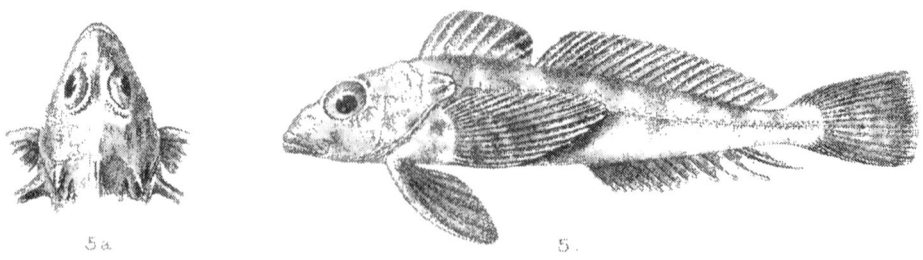

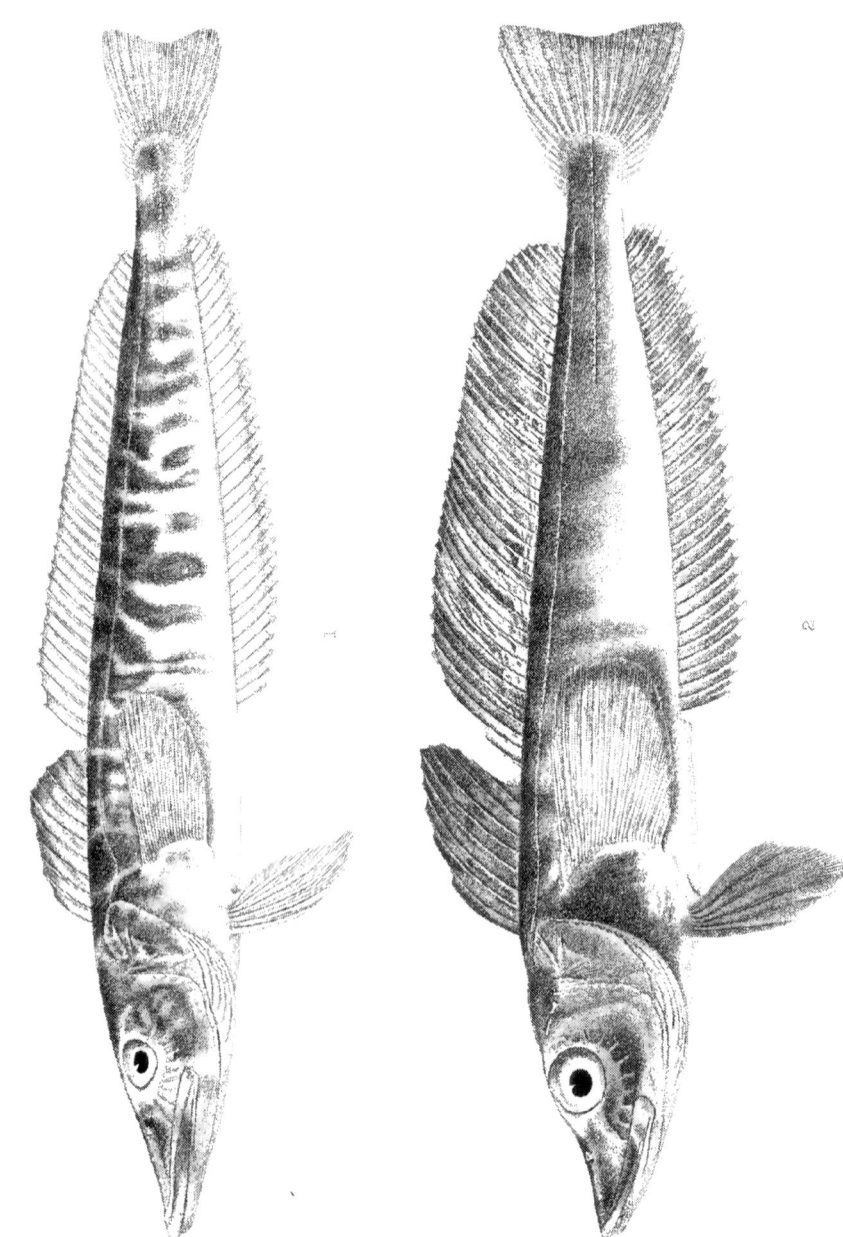

1. CHAMPSOCEPHALUS ESOX. 2. C. GUNNARI.

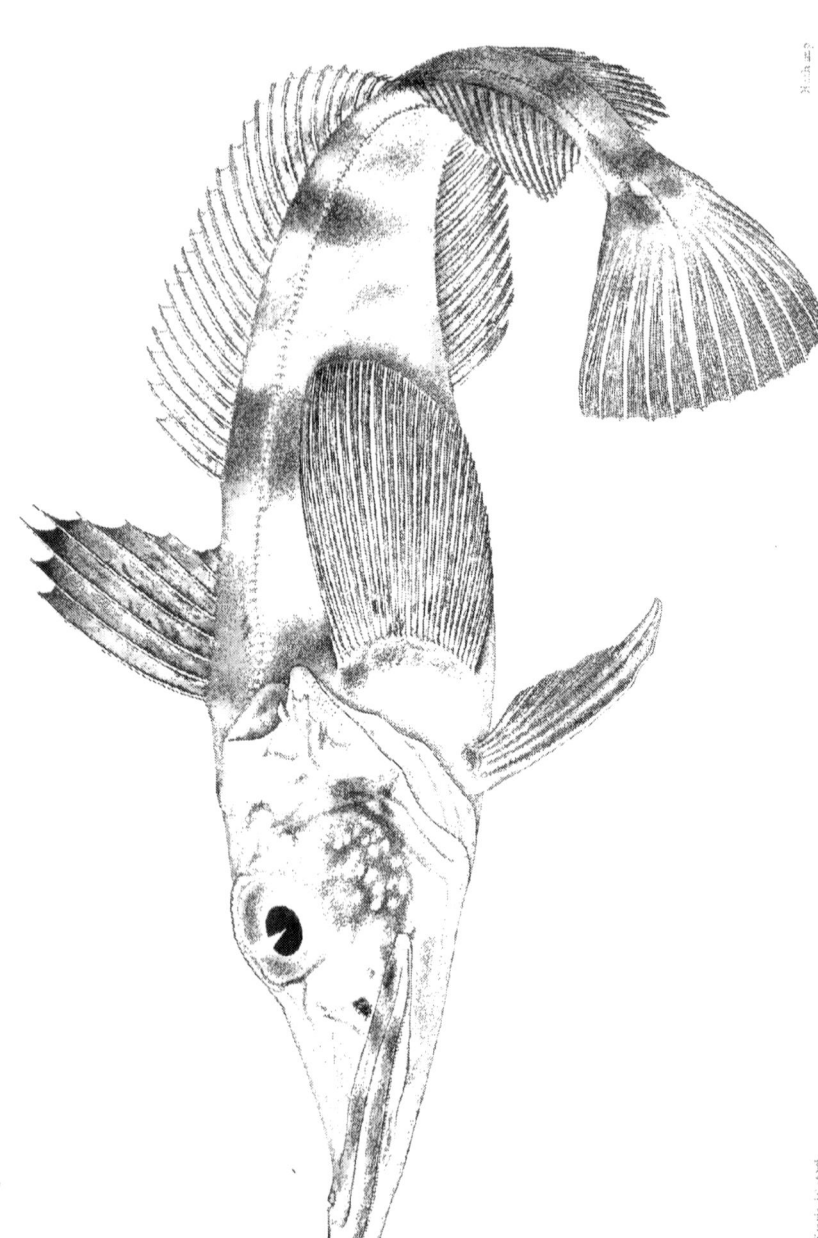

CHAENOCEPHALUS ACERATUS

The TRANSACTIONS of the ROYAL SOCIETY OF EDINBURGH will in future be Sold at the following reduced Prices:—

Vol.	Price to the Public.	Price to Fellows.	Vol.	Price to the Public.	Price to Fellows.
VI.	£0 11 6	£0 9 6	XXXIX. Part 1.	£1 10 0	£1 3 0
VII.	0 18 0	0 15 0	,, Part 2.	0 19 0	0 14 6
VIII.	0 17 0	0 14 0	,, Part 3.	2 3 0	1 11 0
IX.	1 0 0	0 17 0	,, Part 4.	0 9 0	0 7 0
X.	0 19 0	0 16 0	XL. Part 1.	1 5 0	0 19 0
XI.	0 14 6	0 12 0	,, Part 2.	1 12 6	1 5 6
XII.	0 14 6	0 12 0	,, Part 3.	1 6 0	0 19 6
XIII.	0 18 0	0 15 0	,, Part 4.	1 0 0	0 16 0
XIV.	1 5 0	1 1 0	XLI. Part 1.	1 1 0	0 15 9
XV.	1 11 0	1 6 0	,, Part 2.	1 9 6	1 2 0
XX. Part 1.	0 18 0	0 14 0	,, Part 3.	2 5 0	1 13 6
XXII. Part 2.	0 10 0	0 7 6	XLII.	2 2 0	1 11 0
,, Part 3.	1 5 0	1 1 0	XLIII.	2 2 0	1 11 0
XXVII. Part 1.	0 16 0	0 12 0	XLIV. Part 1.	1 18 6	1 9 0
,, Part 2.	0 6 0	0 4 6	,, Part 2.	1 1 0	0 15 9
,, Part 4.	1 0 0	0 16 0	XLV. Part 1.	1 9 0	1 2 0
XXVIII. Part 1.	1 5 0	1 1 0	,, Part 2.	1 7 0	1 0 0
,, Part 2.	1 5 0	1 1 0	,, Part 3.	1 13 9	1 5 3
,, Part 3.	0 18 0	0 13 6	,, Part 4.	0 4 6	0 3 6
XXIX. Part 1.	1 12 0	1 6 0	XLVI. Part 1.	1 1 10	0 16 6
,, Part 2.	0 16 0	0 12 0	,, Part 2.	1 5 8	0 19 4
XXX. Part 1.	1 12 0	1 6 0	,, Part 3.	1 7 3	1 0 11
,, Part 2.	0 16 0	0 12 0	General Index to Vols. XXXV.–XLVI. (1889-1908), with the President's Address delivered at the opening of the New Rooms of the Society, 8th November 1909, etc.		
,, Part 3.	0 5 0	0 4 0			
,, Part 4.	0 7 6	0 5 8			
XXXI.	4 4 0	3 3 0			
XXXII. Part 1.	1 0 0	0 16 0	XLVII. Part 1.	0 19 9	0 15 0
,, Part 2.	0 18 0	0 13 6	,, Part 2.	1 3 0	0 17 4
,, Part 3.	2 10 0	1 17 6	,, Part 3.	1 0 10	0 15 6
,, Part 4.	0 5 0	0 4 0	,, Part 4.	1 7 7	1 0 9
XXXIII. Part 1.	1 1 0	0 16 0	XLVIII. Part 1.	1 2 9	0 17 2
,, Part 2.	2 2 0	1 11 0	,, Part 2.	1 9 6	1 2 5
,, Part 3.	0 12 0	0 9 6	,, Part 3.	1 11 0	1 3 3
XXXIV.	2 2 0	1 11 0	,, Part 4.	0 16 8	0 12 6
XXXV.*Part 1.	2 2 0	1 11 0	XLIX. Part 1.	0 7 6	0 7 6
,, Part 2.	1 11 0	1 3 6			
,, Part 3.	2 2 0	1 11 0			
,, Part 4.	1 1 0	0 16 0			
XXXVI. Part 1.	1 1 0	0 16 0			
,, Part 2.	1 16 6	1 7 6			
,, Part 3.	1 0 0	0 16 0			
XXXVII. Part 1.	1 14 6	1 5 6			
,, Part 2.	1 1 0	0 16 0			
,, Part 3.	0 16 0	0 12 0			
,, Part 4.	0 7 6	0 5 8			
XXXVIII.Part 1.	2 0 0	1 10 0			
,, Part 2.	1 5 0	0 19 0			
,, Part 3.	1 10 0	1 3 0			
,, Part 4.	0 7 6	0 5 8			

Ben Nevis Vols.

* Vol. XXXV., and those which follow, may be had in Numbers, each Number containing a complete Paper.

January 1913.—Volumes or parts of volumes not mentioned in the above list are not for the present on sale to the public. Fellows or others who may specially desire to obtain them must apply direct to the Society. As the Society reprints from time to time parts of its publications which have become scarce, the absolute correctness of this list cannot be guaranteed beyond this date

TRANSACTIONS
OF THE
ROYAL SOCIETY OF EDINBURGH.

VOLUME XLIX PART II

2 *The Antarctic Fishes of the Scottish National Antarctic Expedition* By C TATE REGAN, M A, Assistant in the British Museum (Natural History) *Communicated by* Dr W S BRUCE (With Eleven Plates and Six Text-Figs) Price to Public, 8s, to Fellows, 6s (*Issued May* 23, 1913)

[*For Prices of previous Volumes and Parts see page 3 of Cover*]

www.ingramcontent.com/pod-product-compliance
Ingram Content Group UK Ltd.
Pitfield, Milton Keynes, MK11 3LW, UK
UKHW021545030325
4829UKWH00042B/1503